DIS**CONNECTED**
RE**CONNECTED**

Brick of Gold Publishing Company
New York City
2018

WORDS
UNCAGED

www.wordsuncaged.com
@wordsuncaged

Printed in the United States of America
First Printing

ISBN 978-0-692-13198-5

Designed by Alec Strickland
Cover design by Danny Dwyer
Photographs by F. Scott Schafer

Brick of Gold Publishing Company
New York, NY

thebrickofgold@gmail.com
@brickofgold

Contents

DISCONNECTED - PART ONE

RECONNECTED - PART TWO

A Letter from the Editors

For the past year, a group of us graduate students from Cal State University, Los Angeles' English department have been working with prisoners at Lancaster State Prison in Los Angeles County to produce this book. The men in Lancaster are part of a writing program implemented by Words Uncaged, a non profit organization providing platforms to create dialogue between inmates and the outside world. There are nearly 400 men in the program at Lancaster. Thirty contributed to this project.

The founder and director of Words Uncaged is our professor, Dr. Bidhan Roy. Every Thursday, Dr. Roy would go to Lancaster to see the men and collect their work, and the following Wednesday evening, at Holy Grounds Coffee & Tea, a café just a mile away from CSULA, we would get together to review their writing. We spent many, many hours at the cafe reading the men's submissions, choosing our favorite pieces, and corresponding with them about edits and revisions. We have also spent time writing letters with prisoners outside of Lancaster, helping Dr. Roy plan the annual Words Uncaged art show, and organizing a new writing workshop at a woman's prison in Corona, CA. But our primary task was to curate this collection - the second annual journal from Words Uncaged.

Dr. Roy began preparing us for this project early on. He kicked off the semester with several reading recommendations for the group, providing a ton of different articles on topics like Critical Pedagogy and Participatory Action Research. He told us pick out what we wanted and read as much as we could. We ended up reading quite a few, including a good portion of Paulo Freire's Pedagogy of the Oppressed.

Eventually, the message of these works began to sink in. Through these articles, we learned we were not there to teach these men how to write or to make sure their writing came out "graduate student approved;" we were there because these men had something to teach us and our communities, and we needed to make sure they were heard. In a sense, we were not teaching them. They were teaching us.

As the work started pouring in around the middle of the semester, we were blown away by the men's already developed talent as writers. Our project, then, was less to edit than to revise the pieces. We made recommendations about the structuring of their work or asked them to expand on certain moments in their stories. We tried to see ourselves as sounding-boards for the men, here to provide an ear so they could gage how their words and thoughts were being interpreted.

But what has been most important to us as editors has been to make sure the voices of these men were preserved. As we came across words like "gonna" or "'cuz," or unusual syntactical or grammatical choices, we were faced with the decision to "fix," or to not. Often, we felt it better to not. We believe the writing choices the men made give them something many of us have been searching for our whole writing careers: style. Recognizing the importance of not only what these men are saying, but how they are saying it, has been at the core of our methodology as editors.

We sincerely thank you, and hope the experience of reading the work in this collection is as impactful for you as it has been for us.

- CSULA English Department Grad Students

Preface

For four years I have been visiting Los Angeles County Prison in Lancaster on an almost weekly basis, teaching classes, sitting in on prisoner-led workshops, working with the Paws for Life dog program, producing the WordsUncaged journal and, most importantly, listening to the men imprisoned there. During this time, talk of criminal justice reform and mass incarceration has increasingly found its way into public conversations, both via celebrity voices, as well as via bipartisan supported political reform bills. All of this is a good thing but, sometimes, as I sit in an empty prison yard during count waiting for class to begin, it crosses my mind that, perhaps, such justice reform talk is asking the wrong questions—or, rather, asking questions that are too small. Looking out at the men as they re-emerge from their cells—hundreds of them here, and millions of others like them throughout the country—a bigger question comes to mind: is this what justice looks like? Is this absurd, tragic, institution of prison what we are reforming? Or do we need to ask bigger, more fundamental questions than those of justice reform: questions of what justice is—or might be—and how it functions in our society? Perhaps what we need is a broader public conversation about our views of justice? Questions of the purpose of justice? Whom it serves? And how different stakeholders respond to such questions?

These are philosophical questions that have been asked by thinkers from Plato to Foucault; they are political questions in which discourses of being "tough on crime" and "law and order" have shaped our perspectives; and they are cultural questions in which many of our ideas of justice come from films or television shows that frequently stoke fear in us or offer us neatly gift-wrapped conclusions. They are, of course, also legal questions—but to most of us the opaqueness of legal jargon can lead to passively leaving such issues to lawyers and judges to take care of, thereby abdicating our responsibility as citizens to create the sort of society that we wish to live in. And, while jurisprudence may be a concern for certain law professors, scholars and judges, it is not for most lawyers who are too busy applying laws to specific cases to ponder the bigger questions of what their profession is doing to human lives.

Today in America, many of our responses to questions of justice hinge upon conceptions of punishment and reformulated ideas of vengeance. Turn on your TV, or go to a movie, and this logic inevitably plays out—a man gets his daughter kidnapped and hunts and kills the perpetrators; a king is betrayed and seeks revenge on his betrayers; a person is killed and war declared upon the killers. There is a seductive symmetry to thinking of justice as an equal measure of retribution to the perpetrator of a crime, as we so often see in popular culture; a neat balance of the scales of justice. This logic of retribution is also shared by street gangs who initiate tit-for-tat drive-by shootings, by the Mafia and drug cartels who retaliate by ordering hits on rivals, by Achilles' quest for revenge in the *Iliad*, and by the lone vigilante justice of *Dirty Harry*. Many of the incarcerated people you will read in this book previously subscribed to this logic and, for some, it landed them in prison. But while these forms of punishment are illegal because the American state has a monopoly upon how punishment is administered and who is allowed to perpetrate violence, the underlying logic behind these types of "street justice" often bear uncanny similarities to what we witness in our current legal system: that justice = punishment. Whether we punish through a death penalty, torture, or a life without the possibility of parole sentence, or whether we temper punishment through mercy—we are simply changing the style and degree to which we administer it; we do not radically alter the underlying approach to justice. Indeed, so enmeshed are our conceptions of justice and punishment today that it is incredibly difficult to think what a non-punishment centered justice might look like: justice = punishment often appears to us as "common sense," or even "natural"—a universal concept that is almost unimaginable to think beyond.

But if justice is not conceived through forms of legal punishment, then what? What would replace it? What might other forms of justice look like? What would they feel like? How might we begin imagining them? Can we question the dominant narrative of prison as a necessity that keeps the public safe from harm, how various financial interests are implicated in motivating law enforcement expansion, and how criminalization and imprisonment filter through every aspect of how we live and understand ourselves and the world? Can we imagine a justice in which punishment is not central but in which repairing damage and social peace are? Can we imagine a justice in which both victims and perpetrators do not bury the pain caused by acts of violence but attempt to confront it, and move beyond it—a restorative approach to justice? Can we challenge our stereotypes of who criminals are? Can we challenge our neat categories of criminals and victims, by understanding how those in prison were often also victims of violent crimes themselves? Can we imagine a legal system that does not reproduce trauma but that promotes healing? Can we imagine responsibility toward the victims of violent crimes long after a sentencing hearing has ended? Can we imagine a group of prisoners with life, and life without the possibility of parole sentences, coming together to address the harm that they have caused and attempting to make amends? Can we imagine a process of justice that involves all stakeholders, and that transforms the traditional relationship between communities and their governments in responding to crime?

If you are ready to try to engage with these questions, then read on: this book invites you to join the incarcerated writers, victims of violent crimes, and family members of both, within its pages, to imagine how individual and collective healing is possible when unspeakable traumas are spoken, when hidden scars are exposed, when the burden of pain is shared, when new narratives of self are imagined, and when are we (re)connected to our common humanity. The men, women and children in this book have swam in dark, deep, waters to find these stories and poems and share them with you, so that we might begin to heal individual lives and imagine new collective futures together: such a process is not a spectator sport—step into our circle of healing...

- Dr. Bidhan Chandra Roy

Sitting In The Fire
Christian Branscombe

DISCONNECTED
Part One

Eden is No More

Samual Nathaniel Brown

They have been here before, but this time it is different. He finds it necessary to hold her and assure her that everything will work out for the best. She is fully aware of the fact that as he offers up those few words of encouragement. He himself is not convinced. Still and all she is happy to have him there and he is happy to be there.

Her water broke. They rushed to the local parish hospital where all of the other poor people went for emergencies, surgeries, and miscellaneous procedures. She, Betty. He, John. They were a young African-American couple born and raised in New Orleans, Louisiana.

At home, they had two children anxiously awaiting their return. This latest addition would make three. If things had turned out differently, this baby would actually be their sixth. For this reason, the hospital room was inundated with a mixture of optimism, fear, and uncertainty.

Previously, Betty had a miscarriage with a baby girl. Shortly thereafter, she successfully gave birth to twin baby boys. The twins succumbed to crib death only hours after leaving the hospital. Thus, a lot was riding on this latest child and, as I absorbed nutrients via the umbilical, I also felt the heavy weight of tremendous expectations riding on my tiny shoulders. Expectations from a gigantic world, I had only seen through the emotions of my mother. She needed me. She needed me to be strong. She needed me to be strong and intelligent. She needed me to be strong and intelligent and healthy.

My mother needed me to be an affirmation that she was a good person; a person that was not cursed. Most of all, she needed me to affirm that she was a woman; one not so damaged from life's twists and turns that she could still bring forth life – not death – from her womb. I would not disappoint her. I already loved her too much. I just wanted to hug her and console her so badly that I kicked, punched, tossed, and turned. That was all that I could do to let her know, *I am here for you and I am ready to help you in any fashion that I can.* She made a promise to God that if her pregnancy were to be a successful one, immediately upon my birth, she would relinquish me to him for his bidding.

Yearning to be the panacea for all of her insecurities and uncertainties, my heart beat faster and faster as it filled with anticipation. I vowed that her hurt, her fears, would always be my motivation for both internal and external positive transformation. Once my promise was recorded in the Divine Book of Purpose and

Deeds, I said to God, "I'm ready," and at 7:34 a.m. on February 25, 1977, I was born. My mother named me Samual, which means "God has heard."

I guess it is safe to say that a person cannot know something is different until they first know something other. Growing up in New Orleans, I did not really know how different it was because I had never experienced any place other. As a child, I did not truly understand the unique historical and cultural ingredients that combined to make New Orleans into the gigantic pot of spicy gumbo that it has become known for producing. Instead of rice, cayenne pepper, hot sausage, and blue crab, this gumbo is comprised of the French Constitution, the 1811 Revolt of enslaved African people (the biggest in US history), and unrelenting poverty. Additional ingredients include the rich traditions, the amalgamation of the African and Choctaw Native American bloodlines, the African and French bloodlines, and the French and the Choctaw bloodlines, (ironically) the deeply rooted racism, and the strong spiritual tent overlapping the entire region.

In New Orleans, people practice Voodoo, Ile Ifa, Judaism, Tarot Cards, Islam, Sikhism, Jainism, Buddhism, native belief systems, and all forms of Christianity ranging from Episcopalian to Baptist and Pentecostal. My mom raised me as the latter, Pentecostal that is. The Jerusalem Church of God in Christ was located on the corner of Martin Luther King Jr. Boulevard directly across the street from the murderous Calliope Housing Projects. MLK Boulevard was loaded with housing projects and dilapidated homes from end to end. It was where the dream became a nightmare. Nevertheless, the point being, spirits blanketed the city; those living and just beyond the realm of living. New Orleans was definitely different.

The neighborhood that I was born and raised in was the infamous Ninth Ward of Hurricane Katrina fame. However, long before its recognition for being neglected by George W. Bush in 2005, it had already been neglected long ago by the entire universe. At least, that is how I saw it. To me, my neighborhood resembled every other Third World country that I had ever seen on television. As a youth, I was unable to see much difference between the Ninth Ward and Haiti, the Ninth Ward and Somalia, or the Ninth Ward and Ethiopia. The saddest part, I guess, is I had concluded that this was how all black people lived worldwide.

The Ninth Ward was home to the largest housing projects in the world, the Desire Projects. The Desire Projects were larger than the Queens Bridge Projects in Queens New York and the Cabrini Greens Projects in Chicago, Illinois. My entire neighborhood was black. What I mean by that is the mailman, the alderman, the crack dealer, the crack addict, the corner store owner, the candy house operator, the taxi driver, the pimp, the whore, the school teacher, deacon, missionary, and the preacher – all black, and seemingly poor. You know who was not all black, or even close? The police.

I don't know who negotiated the terms of the agreement, but it appeared that the overall arrangement was that the blacks were to remain on their side of town and the whites would remain on their side of town. Anyone who was not white identified as black, and the wrong person on the wrong side at the wrong time would be made aware of that fact, immediately. This awareness manifested in many forms ranging from icy stares and harsh words to physical assaults and possibly murder. Somewhere along the line, I concluded that all of America was this way. That is to say, this was the true face of America. The world was a ghetto and black people were at the bottom of the totem pole. I did not like it, but somehow I still loved New Orleans.

Before I began to realize these harsh realities, I was just like all of the other children born into the world - teeming with optimism, innocence, and unlimited belief in my potential to conquer the unconquerable, achieve the unachievable, attain the unattainable, and make possible the impossible. I believed that if I concentrated my energy and focused my attention that I could tap into my innate superpowers and I would be able to fly, move objects with my mind, lift automobiles, and the greatest power of all - love, and be loved, by all people. When my parents brought me home from the hospital, I did not know anything about hate, racism, segregation, poverty, domestic violence, sexual abuse, drug abuse, drug dealing, emotional illiteracy, or uncertainty. However, it would not take long for me to learn.

To me, our little duplex was a mansion. Our 1976 Nova was a Mercedes Benz and my two-parent household was the stuff that some people's dreams were made of, including my own. I remember watching my mother and father and revering them as if they were gods. They fed me, bathed me, clothed me, made me laugh, soothed me when I cried, talked to me, and gave me toys to play with.

When I was five years old, Eden began to spoil. Prior to my birth my father had done two tours in Vietnam as a distinguished member of the 101 1st Airborne Screaming Eagles Division. He would parachute into the fiercest of firefights and begin killing countless men that he'd never saw before as fast as he could. The life expectancy of my father and his fellow soldiers was sixteen seconds from the moment that their boots touched the soil. Sixteen seconds! Something else that I did not know about when my parents brought me home from the hospital was Post Traumatic Stress Disorder and its capacity to destroy seemingly perfect family units.

I slept in the bed with my mother and father. It terrified me to be startled awake by them. He – thrashing around and yelling, "No, he's going to kill you! No, no, noooo!" She – equally terrified as she fought to help him realize that he was safe and that we were not the enemy. Yep, Eden was spoiling. The leaves on the Tree of

Life were withering away. My Mom saw the signs, but bound by love and the edicts of Christianity, she would not veer off the road.

I remember when I was around six years old, my father came home yelling at my Mom and they began arguing. Before I knew it, he grabbed her by the arm and forced her into the bedroom. Once the door closed the yelling intensified and there were the sounds of domestic violence - crying, thumping bodies against the walls and door, breaking glass, and finally the three of us children wide-eyed, horrified, and banging on the door while wailing at the top of our lungs.

Eventually, my father came out. When he did, I began to hit his legs with both hands and admonish him about never hitting my Mom again. He backhanded me to the floor and just like that, there went my first attempt at protecting my mother. Feeling like a failure, I fell to the floor and cried. I remember my Mom scooping me up and telling him to never hit me again. He yelled at her and she got quiet. I was confused. I could not understand why the gods were fighting and destroying our family. Was it something that I did? Was it something that I did not do? Was it my fault? Was I supposed to hate the one and love the other? Should I hate them both? Hate myself? I did not know. I did know that I was extremely confused and... angry and... I did hate myself. Withering leaves begin to give way to fallen branches.

In addition to my father being plagued by PTSD, he also began accusing my mother of cheating on him. One night he woke my Mom from a deep sleep with a semi-automatic Colt .45 in her mouth and began interrogating her. He wanted to know who she really was, what she had been doing, and with whom. As the tears rolled down her face, she frantically searched his face hoping to connect with her friend, her lover, her warrior, her protector, her husband that she knew resided within; she tried to answer his questions with that big ole gun in her mouth. I sat in wide-eyed terror observing in silence. I guess she said what he needed to hear because he did not kill her, at least not that night.

The next night, I was once again startled from my sleep. This time, my Mom woke my father up with a .38 revolver in his mouth. She was crying, and I was scared. My fear was exacerbated exponentially by the fact that my father, who was normally so hard and aggressive, was calm. As his eyes danced across her face searching for his friend, his lover, his backbone, his queen, his wife, and an answer, I could tell he was afraid. Although I was young, I felt this was going to turn out really terrible for my Mom if she did not kill him. One thing was certain - he did not seem so tough at that moment. She told him that she loved him and only him and that they would die together. I did not really understand anything except for, "We will die together," and yep, that freaked me out. However, I guess he got the point because she did not kill him. I don't think either one of them took it into consideration, but the fact of the matter is they were killing me. My emotional literacy was dying.

A year later, my two-parent household officially ended. My Mom was ironing my father's clothes when he came in and started raising hell. After almost three years of this behavior, it was still terrifying to me as the first day that I witnessed it. On the other hand, I guess my Mom had decided that she wasn't going to take it anymore. He accused her of cheating and pushed her. In one swift motion, my Mom regained her balance, gripped the iron, and cracked him in the head with it. He went down bleeding profusely. I think my Mom had concluded that if he was not dead, when he got up – she would be. Therefore, she instinctively shifted into autopilot mode.

Even though it seemed like, since I was born, all they did was fight, somehow, they still managed to have two other children together. Therefore, after my Mom busted my father's head with the iron, she tossed my big sister Marie, who was thirteen at the time, the car keys and told her to go crank it up. She had my big brother Torrance, who was twelve at the time, place a few items into the car along with me, and my younger sister Jondana who, at five, was two years younger than I was. My Mom then came running out of the house with my two year old sister Shenise in her arms and a bag full of items that she felt were important (birth certificates, shot records, etc...). As she jumped into the driver's seat and handed Shenise to Marie, my father stumbled to the front door of the house covered in blood and holding his head. Like a scene from an action-packed blockbuster, she frantically threw it into reverse and backed from the driveway so vehemently that sparks probably flew from the undercarriage as the car hit the street with a thud. She then slapped it into drive and literally burned rubber as she mashed the pedal to the metal. As we sped off, I looked out of the back window and as the image of my father grew smaller and smaller into the distance, I knew it was official - Eden was no more.

From that day forth, I always remembered my Mom working two, maybe three jobs to take care of us. Working so many jobs had advantages and disadvantages. On one hand, she made enough money to provide for us. On the other hand, she was not around that often and when she was, she would be dog-tired.

Just my luck, I was the spitting image of my father. Resembling him only served to bolster my self-hate. By this time, I had grown content with telling myself that I hated him. I disliked and resented any adult that called me "Lil John", "his twin", or who claimed that we "looked just alike". I hated that as well. As a result of detesting everything about my father, including the way that he looked, I grew up thinking that I was ugly because people said I looked like him. Unfortunately, it did not stop there.

I grew up feeling rejected, abandoned, and betrayed by him. From the age of seven, I never had a consistent father figure in my life anymore. My uncle Alfred (my Mom's baby brother) lived with us from time to time. His being there served two purposes: babysitting for my Mom and a safe space for him to rest his head. My beautiful, strong mother was wearing both hats and trying to fill all of the voids on her own: nurturer, provider, disciplinarian, teacher, friend, mother, and father. While it was occurring, I did not fully understand this phenomenon, or the phenomenal person that my Mom was. All I saw was red. When I was not seeing red, I was seeing black and white. I was seeing a Cosby Show family or a broken family. I saw me against everybody, the entire universe. Sadly, this also included my mother who was doing all she could to protect me. Nevertheless, I saw the resemblance to my father as the bulk of the reason why she seemed to have a chip on her shoulder towards me.

During these years, ages 7 to 14, lessons were fast, sharp, and deep. My mom was a serious Christian woman. On Monday night, Wednesday night, Friday night, Saturday morning, Sunday morning, and Sunday night, I was in church. Every moment not spent in school was spent in church. That was the primary rule and the other rules that accompanied it were as follows… Drinking, not allowed. Smoking, not allowed. Drug use, of any type, not allowed. Criminal activity, do not even think about it. None of these rules, however, governed my Uncle Alfred. He never went to church and he was always "high". In fact, none of my Mom's brothers or sisters functioned under these guidelines. At their homes, drinking, smoking, cussing, gambling, sex, and Lord knows what else was permissible. My Uncle Alfred did it all. At one point, when I was around nine or ten, we all lived in a house that my great grandfather built after slavery.

My Aunt Gloria and her four children, my mom and her six children, and my uncle Alfred all lived there on Falstoff Street in the Lower Ninth Ward. One night Uncle Alfred came in drunk and high. He passed out on the couch with a lit cigarette on the sofa. The entire house burned down. Fortunately, we were all able to get out of the house safely. Unfortunately, we all had to split up and go our separate ways. My cousins remained in the Lower Ninth Ward, and we moved to the Upper Ninth Ward. Despite the names "upper" and "lower", the entire Ninth Ward was poverty-stricken.

It was during this time that my poor-three-job-working-six-children-raising-every-church-service-attending-two-college-degree-having-mother told me, "If you are ever alone with no adults around and you see the police, run!" She went on to say, "If you can't run, then make sure that you have on the watch I got'chu so you can at least seem like you care what time it is and can pretend like you have somewhere to be." "Why Momma?" I asked. "I ain't done nothing wrong, why I gotta run?" "Cause," she snapped, "You're a young black boy and if the police catch you by yourself, they will kill you baby, or make you disappear and Momma will never see you again. Is that what you want?" "No ma'am," I responded. "Okay then," she said, signaling the end of the discussion. With that said, we had an understanding and I walked away having internalized a visceral lesson.

It would take me many years in prison before I was truly able to grasp why she taught me that. However, at that time, what I did immediately perceive was that the police were the enemy and never to be called upon or trusted under any circumstances. Therefore, I added them to the list of people that I distrusted and disliked. This dislike eventually transformed into full-fledged hate. When I was ten years old, my Uncle Alfred was severely beaten by police officers at a neighborhood liquor store and left bleeding out to die.

Someone ran to our house and told my Mom. She drove to the store and found my uncle there unconscious. The officers had beaten him with their metal batons. Aside from the various scrapes, bumps, and bruises that he had, he was also bleeding from a gash on the side of his head and a gigantic slash across his chest. Witnesses said they busted his chest open with their sticks, but it looked as if he had been slashed with a sword or a box cutter. The cut started at his right shoulder and ended at the bottom of his left pectoral muscle. My Mom rushed him to Charity Hospital. They patched him up and he came home with his head and torso wrapped like a mummy. We all nursed him back to health. The officers were never charged and no one was ever held accountable for what they did to my uncle. That incident confirmed what my Mom had told me about police officers and certified my hate for them. The behavior of my parents, which I perceived to be betrayal against our family, and the KKK-like behavior of law enforcement gave me a long-lasting anti-authority figure mentality.

This beef with authority figures prevented me from being able to see the good in most adults. All I saw was hypocrisy and ulterior motives aimed at controlling me in efforts to further limit my already limited freedoms. This thinking was also rooted in my membership to a sub-culture within a society that told me I could be whatever I wanted to be, yet treated me as if it wished I had never been. The face of this authority figure was the government and I saw it as hypocritical and disinterested in my wellbeing as every other adult and/or person in a position of power.

My Mom had decided that she would allow me to form my own opinions about my father, so she did not really speak down upon him too much. Whenever she was mad at me though, she would threaten to send me go and live with him. Each time she said that it sounded like a punishment, like a banishment. At that time, I still was not sure how to feel about seeing him. On one hand, I swore I hated him. However, in hindsight, that was truly just a coping mechanism for my inability to articulate how I felt about feeling abandoned, inadequate, betrayed, and confused. Moreover, after my Mom clocked him with the iron, the next time that I saw him, I was about eight years of age and seeing him left a sour taste in my mouth. Literally.

He told my Mom that he wanted to take me fishing. She approved. I vaguely remember going fishing with him before and liking it so I was willing to go despite my uncertainty. I no longer recall all of the details from that day. Nevertheless, I will share with you what I do remember. He pulled up and honked the horn for me to come out. I went out and climbed into his truck. During this time, we were living on Star Street in New Orleans East. Specifically, we lived in an area known as Little Woods. Ironically, that is exactly what he did, drove a *little* and pulled over into the *woods*.

I did not think too much about it because the entire area was surrounded by water. The levees held back the waters of the mighty Gulf. We exited the cab and sat on the back of the truck. I am sure that he was using this opportunity to impart some great fatherly wisdom upon his son about masculinity, manhood, friends, family, and survival. Unfortunately, all I remember was him pulling out one of those dwarf six packs of beers, yanking one off, popping the top and telling me, "Drink that." I tasted it and immediately protested, "Uuuhhhh, I don't want to." To which he responded, "Drink all of it." I did as I was ordered, and what did he do? He snatched another one and told me to drink it as well. I did.

I think he handed me a third one and I drank it as well. I don't really know. I woke up in the Lower Ninth Ward at some old woman's house. To this day, I still do not know if she was his grandmother or mine. I imagine that at some point, I threw up, but I honestly do not remember. What I truly remember most about that day was deciding that I hated the smell and taste of beer and I did not want to spend any more time with my father. He was not cool.

Three years later, I found myself with him again. By now, I was familiar with the stories that people told about him. The common theme in all of the stories was that my father was crazy and not one to be messed with. I heard he was a "killer", a "fighter", a "lunatic", and plain and simply off his damn rocker.

Let us see, there was the story about him pulling out a gun and shooting at someone during the middle of a New Orleans Saints game in defense of my mother's older brother, Uncle Junior. Then, there was the time he went to jail for standing in the street and shooting up my Uncle Jabby's house (his own brother) with an M-16. Those were two stories that I had become well acquainted with by the next time that I went to visit him. I had also learned a few about my Mom as well. Like the time she beat a girl down, pinned her to the ground, and scraped the skin off of her face with a red brick. Another tale was of her stomping a girl's face on a curb and splitting her mouth.

The next visit to my father's house found Nana, my baby sister, Nisey, and me all disenchanted about the very idea of going. None of us wanted to be there. I think I did a little bit better at masking it than Nana. Nisey (one of the girls that looked like him, Marie being the other) did not stand a chance. She was only 6 years old and he showered her with attention. He gave me a $20.00 book of food stamps and told me to walk them to the corner store and purchase whatever snacks and junk food we wanted. That night, he made pork'n beans and rice with the cut up hot dogs, bacon, and sugar in it for dinner. We couldn't get enough. After my sisters fell asleep, he said he wanted to show me something and walked me to his bedroom.

Lying on his bed was enough artillery to storm a small village. There were various knives, daggers, rifles, grenades, semi-automatic handguns, revolvers, swords, machetes, nunchakus, a gas mask, a canteen, and intricately designed throwing stars of all sizes. An American flag lay folded atop of his dresser alongside of some green fatigues and a photo of him wearing them with a helmet on his head. I did not really know what to think. I was really impressed by the "ninja stars" (that's what I called them), the swords, and the grenades. I don't recall feeling afraid of him that day. Instead, I felt...proud. I could tell that he felt proud to be sharing this part of him with me as well.

"Do you know what this is?" he asked as he reached for one of the handguns. "Nope." "That's a Colt .45," he said with pride. Then it dawned on me - *that was the gun he had placed in my mom's mouth that night*. I wondered how many people he had killed with it and if he had kept all of these guns in the house back when we all lived together. "This one is also a Colt .45," he said as he picked up a gun identical to the first one. "I call them the twins and I carry them both at the same time." "Why?" I asked. "For protection." I never bothered to ask him from whom it was that he felt he needed protection. Instead, I recall simply feeling like I understood.

"Here, let me see you hold this." He handed me a rifle and as I reached for it, he said, "That's an AK-47. That's the one that you grab when they think they got'chu outnumbered." "Filing these lessons away, I quickly responded, "Okay." "Here, hold this one." I did as I was told. "Okay." This one is an M-16 and it is also good to get the job done if you cannot get to that," he said, referring to the Ak-47. He spent the rest of the night telling me about the weapons and it really caught my attention when he said, "And one day this will all be yours." "Okay." I said, eyeing the ninja stars and liking the idea of one day having a cache of weapons to call my own. "Every man needs a collection like this because one day it is going to come in handy. Remember that alright?" "Alright."

He gave me a set of the throwing stars to keep and I took them home with me. I cannot count how many holes I put into my bedroom walls from throwing those things, especially when I was angry, which was quite often. One time I was so angry that I threw the largest star practically through the closet door. It was not anger as much as it was fury - fury from one of the most traumatic events of my life.

There was a new movie showing that I desperately wanted to see. Unfortunately, the events of that night totally wiped my memory of any recollection of what that movie was. It was the summer of 1988, I was eleven years old, and the movie could have been Boys in the Hood or Gremlins for all I know. I simply do not remember. What I do remember is having to be on extra good behavior and do more than my share of chores for over a week in order to get my Mom to finally agree to me going to see the movie.

Since my Mom would be working at one of her jobs, she arranged for my big sister, Marie, to drop me off, and pick me up afterwards. At around 6 p.m. she dropped me off at the Joy Theater on Canal Street, walking distance from Café Du Monde, Bourbon Street, the Super Dome, and the River Walk. To us locals this area was referred to as the "tourist trap". To this very day there are numerous reports about the multitude of unsolved murders in New Orleans. Many of those unsolved murder cases were of tourist who went to see the sights and either disappeared or were shipped home in a pine box. It is very sad, but it is very true.

The movie ended around 8:30 p.m. I stood outside that movie theater waiting for my sister for a minimum of four hours. The theater closed, the employees left, and the streets emptied of both pedestrians and automobiles. At around 1:00 a.m. I decided to walk home. Most people don't know that outside of the tourist attractions, literally, just outside of them, New Orleans is all ghetto. It is extremely dangerous.

If I were to make a guesstimation, I would say that the Joy Movie Theater was 7 to 10 miles away from our home. There are trees next to the sidewalks and in many of the front yards. The tree canopy combined with the dearth of streetlights make the sidewalks extremely creepy. They were dark, mysterious, and quite frankly not the place to walk - definitely not the place for an 11 year old to be walking at 1:00 in the morning. Therefore, I opted to walk on the neutral ground. In New Orleans, it's pronounced "newtra ground", and it refers to the little strip of land that separates the sides of a street. In California it is known as the "island".

While I was avoiding the sidewalk shadows, basically walking up the middle of the street, a guy in a red car pulled up alongside of me and asked, "Man, what are you doing out here walking down the middle of the street this time a night?" I explained to him that my sister had left me hanging and I needed to get home. When I told him where I stayed he said he was headed that way and offered me a ride. I wasn't afraid, but I was hesitant because I did not know this guy. Sensing my reluctance, he said, "It's up to you, but I don't mind. I really am going that way and it is dangerous for you to be walking like this." I accepted his offer and hopped in.

At first, we rode in silence while I looked out of the window just grateful for a ride. I no longer had to watch the sidewalk shadows. It seemed much more safe and peaceful. He begins to ask me all sorts of questions, stuff like, "What type of music are you into?" and "What sports do you like?" As we neared the intersection that lead to my house he asked, "How old are you?" "Eleven, going on twelve," I answered. He then asked me, "Do you have an older brother?" "Yeah." "How old is he?" "18," I lied. He was really 16, but I wanted him to imagine he was big, strong, and protective of me because I was beginning to get a bad feeling. "Oh," he said as he suddenly placed his hand on my knee and sensually squeezed it. "I should be messing with him, huh?" referring to my big brother. I grabbed his hand and pushed it away with force. Out of nowhere, he backhand punched me right in the left side of my ribs. It knocked the wind out of me. As I recoiled from the pain, he reached for a gun. By the time I caught my breath and looked at him, he had the gun in his left hand pointing at me, and his right hand back on my knee. The car was going slow as he angrily warned me, "Don't ever push me away again!" Then, instantly calmer, he continued. "Just do what I tell you to do and you will be alright." Damn. So much for the peaceful ride - I was kidnapped.

He sped the car up, steered the automobile with his hand that held the gun and placed his hand on my knee once again. As I sat there angry and afraid, he ran his hand up my leg and placed it on my penis and left it there. "You ever been with a man before?" he asked. "No," I responded. "You ever had sex before?" "No." He became excited and through crooked yellow smiling teeth, he looked at me and said, "Wow, I get to be your first! Don't worry I will be gentle." He then removed his hand from my penis and placed it on my thigh.

When we pulled to the stoplight on the corner of Louisa Street and Chef Montour/Franklin Blvd, I told him, "This is my turn right here." He squeezed my thigh and said, "We are going to go to my place first." Directly ahead of us was a big bridge that crossed over the Mississippi River. I told myself that if I crossed that bridge or went to his home, I was dead. My family would never see me alive again. I responded, "Okay." When he pressed the gas pedal and the car sped up, I unlocked the passenger side door and yanked the door handle all in one motion. He must have been doing in between 25 to 30 mph, but I didn't give that any thought.

I dove out of the car, did my best Chucky doll roll, jumped up and compelled by a mixture of mortal fear and pure adrenaline, literally ran for my life. I heard him yell, "Muthafucka!" He backed up, and shot at me twice. My last glance of him locked an image in my head of his face as a contorted mask of anger and rage. I just ran, and ran, and ran...

Once I passed Popeye's and crossed the train tracks, I realized that he was not chasing me. Still, I ran another block. Safely within my neighborhood – which was also very dangerous – I began to walk. While walking, I looked up and on the other side of the street driving at full speed was my sister. I knew she was headed to the Joy Theater to pick me up. When I arrived home, I let myself in, went to my room, and grabbed my ninja stars. I imagined that sucker's face and with all of the fury that I could muster, I threw them deep into the closet door. I then cried angry tears until I fell asleep. I never discussed this incident, or how it made me feel. I buried those feelings that night. Along with those feelings, I officially buried my emotional literacy.

We Never Did Find Out

Dortell Williams

The sun shined as the chilled breeze caressed our 12-year-old slender frames. My brother Darren and I were playing street ball with the other kids while Dad visited our grandmother in the house. Sporting blue jeans and t-shirts, we worked up a sweat running various plays and exercising our skills. Right smack in the middle of the play, Dad emerged from the house. "Let's go fellas!" Darren contorted his body to avoid an Oldsmobile, while making a fantastic mid-air catch. Shouting with the vernacular of the day, we responded, "Man, that was bad!"

"Mothaf…, I said let's go!" Dad's voice boomed!

Sensing his apparent irritation, we dropped everything and trotted toward him. We were embarrassed by his demanding tone in front of our friends. We wondered, *were Dad and Grandma fighting again? Was Grandma drunk and on pills again?* We were too far away to hear the usual discord, the cursing, threats with knives in hand, or Grandma hurling bread rollers across the room for the most trivial of reasons.

"Get in the back of the truck," he bellowed. Darren and I shared a confused look. "We wanted to listen to the radio," I responded, insinuating that we wanted to ride in the cab, the same way we had come. Dad did not relent, "In the back, I said, damn it!" We complied.

As Dad drove through the streets toward home, the cold gnawed at our skin. The gentle breeze now as angry as Dad, biting us to the bone.

Darren and I sat opposite of each other on the wheel wells, watching the other violently shiver. We attempted to wrap ourselves in our own arms, twisting and contorting like pretzels to stay warm. We were desperate to stave off the aching cold that was now the enemy. My brother and I kept looking at one another, like, *What the f.......!* We had no idea what we were being punished for. However, when Dad pulled over into a gas station we both sighed in relief, thinking that he was going to give us a reprieve, perhaps just cursing us out. That would have been a welcomed alternative at that point.

Instead, Dad got out of the truck. He didn't look at us or say anything. He gassed the vehicle. Then, to our utter surprise, he threw water on us from the bucket used for patrons to clean their windshields. We gasped, shocked.

Dad returned to the truck and got on the 405 freeway headed toward Inglewood, home. Darren and I looked at one another again, *What the f...?* The sadness in my brother's eyes made me want to cry. And in retrospect, my eyes were likely a younger reflection of his. We both wanted to cry, but we didn't. Like every other adversity, we internalized it, the intense hurt and pain.

Our happiest moment wasn't when Dad turned on to Hillcrest, our street, or when we saw the house, or even when Dad pulled into the cracked, cement driveway. "Get out," Dad commanded and walked away. That's when we knew it was over.

Darren and I never talked about that day, and I've never ridden in the back of a truck since.

We Never Did Find Out

All Tied Up

Kenneth Webb

It was day one of my trial, seven days after my 20th birthday. "Webb! Do you have anything to wear?" says an officer. "Yeah, my mom should have them," I reply. The officer closes the gate, leaving me to think about how this dreadful day would turn out. I take one long deep breath in hopes of removing some stress. I realize that I'm pacing back and forth. Time is dragging as my county jail karate kicks do the same.

In the midst of my pacing I hear, "Aye bro!"

I look up to see a man sitting in the further corner. I'm not sure how I missed him.

I screw my face and say, "What up, cuhz?"

My gangbanger tough guy voice didn't even make him blink, instead he says, "You look nervous bro."

I'm sure my face shows irritation. *No shit,* I think in my mind. I nod and continue to pace back and forth. I walk in my silence thinking thoughts of the unknown. Before I know it, these thoughts are pressing against my lungs and I feel my breaths getting short, I can't breathe! Mid-step, I drop to a squat, "Shit, shit, shit! I don't want to go in there."

The mysterious corner man walks to me and says, "It's going to be alright youngster, just relax."

I catch my breath then go to the sink to get a sip of water. I drink the tart water, clear my throat, and give an embarrassed, "Thank you," to the corner man.

Moments later, I find myself looking in the small mirror. I look at my youthful face, a few strains of hair making a beard, spotted with bumps like I just started puberty.

The cage door opens, "Webb, here you go, get dressed."

My clothes fly through the door. I take them and stare for what seems like a lifetime. Street clothes, a small token of freedom, the support of my family buying them brings a smile to my face. For a moment I forget why I'm holding these nice clothes. I forget that I shot and killed Eron Mull. I forget that for 2 years, I've been living a life of madness, waiting for this very moment.

I start to get dressed. My pants fit perfect, and so does my shirt. I tuck in my shirt and slide on my belt. I see the tie on the bench and avoid it. Instead, I go for the cashmere sweater and slide it over my slim body. It suddenly hits me, *Trial is going to begin soon,* and I'm terrified. If I could run and hide, I'd bolt for it.

I look back at the tie, reluctant to pick it up. I imagine it is a snake, wrapping itself around my leg, biting me. The venom infecting my body as I drop to my death. I think, *I'd rather die than do life in prison.* I smirk as a voice snaps me out of my childish daydream.

"You ready?" the officer asks.

I shake my head no.

"Why not?" he says, his voice carrying irritation.

He looks at me, and then my tie, "You don't know how to tie it?"

"No," I respond.

There weren't too many people in my life that had a need to wear a tie, yet alone, show me how to tie one.

The officer grabs it and places it around my neck, pity in his eyes, shame in my own. As he finishes the knot, I wonder if he ever foresaw this interaction happening. He pats me on my shoulder, and it strangely feels like a father-son moment. I want to ask him for help out of this mess, but we were 2 people on the opposite sides of the law, and there is no easy way out.

"I'll go see if they're ready for you," he says.

I sit there waiting in the hallway, my emotions and thoughts, all tied up tighter than my tie. I pull on my collar, loosening my tie, just a bit. I take a deep breath before I enter the courtroom. There's no way out.

Remember

Spoon Jackson

When I walk or fly

Out of this place

No one will remember

How the birds came to me

As friends and shared bread

No one will remember

How I planted a garden

Of flowers and spices

In a space where growth is prohibited

No one will remember

The Shakespeare and my poems I read in hostile classes

I should have known

That once the trees

Were all chopped down

Like unarmed soldiers

I would be transferred.

Catechism of Failure (2017)

Daniel Whitlow

Life is more than living—

Fading tendrils of silent smoke slither and curl and climb into night.

These charred remains were once cold, set ablaze by a kiss, and the flames let loose a ghastly howl of triumph as my contorted form was consumed, as tongues of bright fire erupted and bloomed from my skin.

My affliction, it would seem, is the sickness that heals me.

My infection flows a sickly green; sweet acidic jealousy.

No soil can bury me nor can shackles bind—from these smoldering ashes, I will rise, in spite of the staring, sightless eyes and gaunt-faced hollow dim-witted designs that persist as the sole possession of dirt mongers of stupidity who clutch the sanctity of ignorance and filth—broken bloody fingers clinging to the deceiving discriminations of love's impurities.

Skeleton-shrieked in faithless tones of faltering melodies. Companion worms writhe, whispering boiled angels impaled and left to die.

Love goes beyond death— I will bide my time with the patience and pious grace of a faceless god, a statue of flesh, spewing sermons of sinew and sacrifice.

But there is a price to release the flames entombed in ice behind the defeated eyes of every forgotten lover's empty smile.

A committed heart is never free—a catastrophe that is known to me.

Perhaps I am a casualty of hopeful dreams, lost in the deluded, pastoral bliss of what I think I deserve, a distant cry from reality.

Only I am capable of betraying my humanity, and though vile, I will eat of my waste and drink my bile, fashion toothless keys to liberate my disease and resurrect this smoking ruin—

A blackened human knot work forced to its knees.

Lost

Frank Garcia

This is how my freedom ends and life sentence begins. It's mid-February, a dreary day. The dark grey clouds cover the sky like a canopy. The fiery rays of the sun can't penetrate the foreboding emotions of the clouds. I wake at a friend's house, alone. The emptiness of the house adds to my feelings of loneliness inside. Sleep came to me last night, a long lost friend, but I am bone tired and restless. I have a lot on my mind. I am out on bail for a gun possession, and my girlfriend left me.

I am a meth addict, although I haven't gotten high in a couple of days. I am fiending for a hit to get away from my problems. I am trying to get sober. I don't want to live like this anymore, but crystal has been my longest relationship. I first met her when I was 15 years old. Since the first kiss, she's been my constant companion; the cause, and solution, to all my problems. My girl is gone, but crystal is there for me to help pick up the pieces of my broken heart. I just turned 22, and the longest I've been sober was a three-week stint in the county jail. I am in an emotional tornado, spinning out of control, the last few days, I was there, until I found myself in the eye of the storm. It is calm, till shit hits the fan. I don't know how to cope with my broken relationship. How can I have one when my rails are bent and twisted. How could it not be a train wreck?

My life is in shambles. Deep down I know I am the cause of all my problems. I hate myself. I hate how I am living. I don't know who I am anymore. All this stress and anxiety in my mind, I get up and decide that I need a beer. A 40oz. of Budweiser will help settle down my nerves. I go outside and up the block— panic hits me. A car is driving by. I see the driver but there could be someone in the back waiting to jump out. I hide behind a parked car, along the curb till it passes by. Paranoia catches up to me, as I realize that I'm walking naked (without a gun). I know all too well how easy it is to get caught slipping. I have been shot at on many different occasions, I know it can happen any time of the day. The enemy doesn't sleep. With this feeling in my gut, I take a detour and head to an apartment complex where I know my homie stashed a gun. I head to the carport, and in the shelf, I find it. The gun is my role model, a 9mm blue steel, semi-automatic. It's cold, hard, and uncaring. I pull up my hoodie sweater and put it in my waistband.

I feel relief as the fear in my gut is replaced by the sense of security the pistol brings. I begin my trek to the liquor store for the 40. At the least, I drink one a day. I leave the apartment and walk up the block, when a truck roles up. I recognize the bald head of my homeboy, with the eye buster tattoo on his neck.

He's a little older than me, but new to the hood. He has his little brother rolling with him. "What's up, where you going?" he says. "I'm heading to the store for a beer, I feel like shit," I reply. "You look like you ain't slept in a week, foo! Jump in. I'll give you a ride." His name is Mono—Spanish for monkey—and his little brother's name is Triste. I tell Triste "move over," and I sit in the middle. "I'm strapped, in case I gotta jump out," I say. We head up the block, the roar of his engine speeding up echoing down the street. We get to the store and I'm in and out, buying the beer. I jump back in, "Where to?" Mono asks, "Let's go to your old apartments," I say. I just want to get somewhere and drown out my problems. This beer would be the solution. I feel depressed, and gray inside as the clouds above me. The emptiness inside I run from and avoid. I suppress it with alcohol and meth. How do I change my life? How do I get my girl back? How much time am I going to get for this case? I don't want to do the time. I'm sick of this life. I think of all this at the same time, my face stone cold, reflecting none of my inner turmoil.

Mono pulls up in front of the apartments and we get out. We post up in front of a two-story building, white with blue trim, and a mesh fence. We get behind the fence. I get the beer out, but get the urge to use the restroom. I tell the homies to keep point, and holler if anything. I head to the side of the apartment and take a piss. I walk back to the front, and begin to break the seal of the beer. It cracks a couple of times, then I hear the word, "Juras." Right then I stop dead in my tracks, dropping the beer as I see the black and white pull into the driveway. Anger flashes through my mind, *these idiots can't even keep point!* I run, thinking, *I got to get away*. The cops jump out. I'm already running down the side of the apartments. One gives chase, while the other runs down the street. I run like a gazelle runs from a lion. *I gotta get away*! Not again, I don't want to go to jail. I got too many things on my plate already. Adrenaline kicks in. I get to the back of the apartment and jump the wall in one swift motion, as if death himself was on my heels, sickle in hand. I hear the loud clunks of the police officers utility boots getting closer. I can't get caught with another gun. My dad is not going to bail me out this time. *Run! Run! Run!* sprints through my mind. I can get away! I get to the next apartment complex and run down the side of it. *I can do it; I can lose him!* I convince myself. I hear footsteps. He's jumping the wall. I get to the end of the side of the apartment, *fuck, it's a dead end*. There's a recess in the wall where the meters are. I duck in and I'm trapped! Panic blows through my mind.

I'm cornered like a feral dog. My adrenalines pumping with every beat; it's flight or fight. I pull the gun out and point it back where I came from, and fire in rapid succession: one, two, three, four, five, six, seven times. My twisted mind thinks, *this should distract him enough for me to get over the wall.*

Instincts to run kick in, and I run out of the cut toward the wall. I see the officer at the end of the pathway, on the ground and in a sitting position, his radio scattered on the floor, the garbled static coming out of it. I reach the wall and try to jump it. He pulls his gun out from his belt and opens fire. I see the muzzle flash. Boom, Boom, Boom, eight times. Bullets whizzing past me like angry bees. The magazine is spent. The sound reverberates off the building as I reach for the top of the wall, pulling myself up. He reloads and opens fire again. I feel bullets cutting through the air against my skin as the hot metal sizzles by. I'm almost up the wall. Everything is in slow motion. I feel the impact of the rounds exploding, concrete chunks of rocks flying into the air like shrapnel, hitting my face. I smell dust in the air. I finally pull myself over the wall and my feet touch the ground. "Which way do I go?" I run right, and there's a black, gated fence in my way. *Fuck! What did I just do? Why did I shoot this fucking gun? I gotta get rid of it. I can't get caught now.* I run along the fence, open the gate, and begin running to the corner. I hear, "FREEZE!" coming from 20 feet behind me. I turn around to look and feel a bullet fly past my ear. The whizzing sound of wind blowing by, followed by another explosion. This time I feel the hot metal pierce through my sweater and burn into my flesh. It enters with burning hot quickness, like the devil's hot fingertip poking into me. I feel his tendril weaving into my body, like a snake thirsty for blood. I stop dead in my tracks and turn to look at the officer who just shot me. "What the fuck are you doing?" I say. I put my hands in the air so he can see that I don't have the gun in hand. He gives me a puzzled look and stops shooting.

Instincts kick in again. *I got to get away!* I begin to run, I gotta ditch the gun. I grab it and throw it into the grass on the sidewalk, thinking at least they won't shoot me anymore if I don't have the gun. *You're a fucking idiot! What did you do?* I try to run on, but the bullet that hit me went into my back by my armpit, at an angle, and entered my body going through a lung. It's working its way through my chest, barely missing my heart, embedding itself in my sternum. I taste metal. *Why do I taste pennies?* The bitter copper taste comes in a flood, gushing up out of my throat. I'm gasping for breath. It feels like I am trying to blow up a balloon that has a hole in it. After a few steps I know I can't go on. I collapse on the ground and begin to wheeze. I can't breathe, I can't catch my breath. There, on the ground, a strange calmness comes over me. *Finally, I'll get some rest from this life. I hope I am forgiven.* A police officer yells, "DON'T MOVE. DON'T MOVE!" He slams his knee into my back, pulls my arms back, and cuffs me.

As I'm lying there, the stillness envelopes me. I feel at peace, even though I'm drowning in my own blood. A fitting end to my life of reckless abandon. Laying on my stomach, wheezing, I look up to the dark sky and think, *God, if your there, am I going to die?* I feel no pain... I feel nothing... I am nothing... I feel the first drops of rain splashing on my face, a light pitter-patter against my skin. Could this be God's response to my question? The cleansing rain, washing away the foul stain of my sinful life.

A police officer comes up to me and asks me what happened. He looks familiar. He's an officer that has arrested me before. I've known him throughout my teenage years. "I'm fucked. I'm shot," I say, every word coming out a guttural sound. The pain of my wound is now in full bloom. "Who was it?" he asks. "I'm sorry," is all I can say. I am drowning. I can feel and hear a gurgling sound in my chest. In an instant, I'm being carried and put on a gurney. *Who are these people helping me? Why do they care?* They begin cutting my clothes off, first my sweater and shirt, then my pants. They're examining my body, asking where I was shot. I'm past being able to speak. All I can do is point. I try to tell them I can't breathe, but it comes out a gurgling noise. They put me in an ambulance. The doors shut, sounding like a coffin being closed. There's a woman with light brown hair who has a concerned look on her face, as if in deep thought. I never got the chance to know her name. She orders me to put my right arm above my head, and to take a deep breath. I do what she says, and at the apex of my breath, there's a loud thud in my side, then an explosion of pain in my rib cage. She stabs me through muscle and bone, tearing into my body with a metal tipped tube. As it punctures my lung, I feel blood gush out like a volcanic eruption. Instantly, my lung expands with the release of the blood. I gasp as the sweet relief of life fills my body. *Am I going to live? I'm tired... I just want to rest...* I black out...

I'm in and out of consciousness at the hospital, with doctors standing over me, and people shouting. *Am I dreaming?* I wake up in a daze, then sheer panic overwhelms me. I feel a tube going down my throat; I'm hooked up to a machine that is breathing for me. I began to gag, "Get it out! Get it out!" I reach for the tube, but I'm unable to. My hands are handcuffed to the bed. *Calm down,* I tell myself. As the panic subsides, memories begin flooding in. The realization of what I have done hits me like a ton of bricks. *Am I dreaming?* I ask myself. *Am I really alive? Is this hell?* I begin looking around, and see two police officers watching me, laughing and smiling. One of them gives me a look with hate in his eyes, and flips me off. As days go by, and the weight of my actions bare down on me, I realize that life is precious. I took so much for granted. I was afraid to grow up. I ran from any kind of responsibility. Whatever life threw at me, I avoided. I hid in a cloud of smoke, too scared to face my feelings.

There's a window next to my bed with a view of a park, the park I grew up at. I can see its familiar lights, as memories of my childhood flash in my mind. I remember my small body swinging on those rusty swings, kicking my feet to go higher and higher. It was a carefree time, with my family and friends, eating tortas from the taco truck. Fond memories become heavy burdens, as I realize I will never see that park again. All that is in store for me is concrete walls, and fences with barbed wire. My heart drops, now I know what freedom means. I think of the irony of it all. Now that I see the answers to my life, I will never be free to make it right. I shake my head, take a deep breath, and close my eyes... waiting for my new life to begin.

Fences

Lester Polk

The urge was irresistible. From the time I was twelve, whenever I would see a fence I had to climb it. It didn't matter if it was chain link, wooden picket or brick Masonite. If it was six, eight or ten feet tall. In fact, the higher, the better. In my young mind, a fence was a barrier to the happiness that would fill me when my thirst for adventure was satiated, when I knew the unknown of what lay on the other side.

Growing up as a fat kid, I was always left behind but that sad truth changed when I found I had a knack for "hitting" fences. Peer pressure and my quest to find love and acceptance to fill my life's fatherless void added to my drive. It was never a question of if I would go over a fence; it was how many of my friends I would beat. I'd even get the edge on the most agile guy in my crew. I think it was because I didn't care much about myself that I was a able to complete this feat with such reckless abandon. Fence-jumping turned into a rite of passage that positioned me in my group's social structure. While I wasn't the alpha dog, I sure wasn't the runt of the litter anymore.

Growing older, I would venture out of my comfort zone to wealthier, more sophisticated neighborhoods. In my mind, I was trying something new in the name of broadening my horizons, but in my truth, I was running—running far away from a single mother drowning in the turbulent waters of raising a man, far away from my father's rejection, far away from poverty, and far away from my own inferiorities. I ran and ran until I reached a place where physical and sexual abuse did not exist, to a place where I could wake up from a seemingly never-ending nightmare.

My weekends brought freedom from the Möbius strip that I lived in as I escaped into a hunt for adventure. What had started as a shortcut to adventure became the adventure itself. Many times the rewards were absolutely amazing. I discovered a brave new world with neat, members-only basketball courts and manicured golf courses. I discovered glimmering swimming pools that provided sweet refreshment in the blistering summer heat. I found fruit trees teeming with all kinds of ripe pickings.

I was never much of a basketball player but as a black kid from the ghetto, I had to handle to rock. So when I found a secluded court with painted lines, a clean backboard and a new net, I brought my faded, worn leather ball foreign to this virgin terrain, and the hoops were on!

Unlike in the movies, there was no grisly old groundskeeper to shoo me off, but occasionally I'd run into a member or a staffer who would look at me pityingly, I loved and hated those looks. Loved because sometimes this entailed a spectacular acrobatic feat of jumping at the top of a chain-link fence and flipping my body over, hopefully landing on my feet. This maneuver, of course, wasn't always performed with cat-like charm and agility. There were many sprains, scrapes and lasting breaks, none of which hindered me until the adrenaline wore off.

At the dawn of my mid-teens, I became too old to run through neighbors' yards or to sneak into off-limits areas. I still ran away from the Möbius strip but now I was hitting figurative fences instead. I would break curfew. I would drive like I knew no mortality and, with the advent of puberty, have sex like I knew no morality.

Most thought these exploits were youthful hijinks, but they were more than that. They sowed in me a seed that would grow into a total disregard for authority. For some teenagers, that may mean playing loud music and using disrespectful language. For me, it meant a drive to obtain material goods as fast as possible to add value to what I deemed a worthless life and to compensate for traumas I had no idea how to address.

As a kid, I'd say, "Fences are meant to be climbed," but the message that registered subconsciously was, "Rules are made to be broken." Little did I know back then that those fences were not there to keep me from my happiness, but to keep me from my own despair. They prevented me from getting in trouble. Hated because they exposed my station in my life.

I especially loved the golf courses because, of course, I wasn't supposed to be in these oases of affluence. I didn't like golf, but I liked doing snow angels in the sand traps. I never got caught because I had latched on to a hustle. I would sell geriatric businessmen their balls back. They were so entitled that they assumed I was the help.

The pools were different. No one wanted me in their pool. Compassion be dammed, and with good reason, since I didn't respect the value of it. I just wanted to cool off. I didn't care if I wore my shoes in the pool or made a mess. I only cared about running if the owner came home.

Backyard fruit trees were another lure. One of our favorites were blackberries but the thorny bushes meant that only those who had gall could get them. Of course, that meant me. Unlike apples or bananas, the berries not only marred my hands and clothes with purple juice, but also my acceptance for what was normal and regular. They left me wanting to always get what was better and more desired so I'd be viewed as better and more desired.

Other times, my spirit of adventure paid off no better than the antics of Curious George, and my findings were more punishment than reward: angry Rottweilers and surprised homeowners who threatened us with loud curses. The fence would then become an adrenaline fueled escape route to shake the cops, who could care less about a trespassing minority kid anyway.

Now incarcerated, I find myself surrounded by two miles of chain- link fence topped with coils of razor wire and threaded with 10,000 volts of electricity, I can't help but wonder if there's a younger version of me wanting to hit the fence. If I could, I'd tell him there's nothing in here to see.

A Knife, A Nightclub, and Juvenile Hall

Justin S. Hong

What the fuck have I done. After spending hours in the police station taking mug shots and cuffed to a bench, I am on my way to Central Juvenile Hall in Los Angeles. Hands cuffed behind my back, I brace my feet as the police car makes a sharp turn. Still, I slide and have to reposition myself on the hard-plastic seat. The dried blood caked on my face smears as I try to wipe it off with my knee. *What the fuck have I done.*

My night started with plenty of promise. I was hanging out with Christina, a girl I liked. I remember the first time we met, she sent one of her friends to profess her interest in me like an elementary school crush.

"She thinks you're really cute," her match-making friend said.

"Really?" I was flattered and incredulous.

It wasn't long before we were talking late into the night and intertwining our weekends.

Hours before I ended up in a police car, Christina was nestling against my chest, warming the cold night air. I could smell the sweet scent of her shampoo as we cozied up against a car in a parking lot beside my house. A phone call from my older homie Sam interrupted our cuddling. He was at the nightclub, Karnak, a few blocks away. The beat of loud music and buzzing in the background distorted his voice. "I'm here—with the girls. Give me another shot! Hurry up— just hurry up and stop by!"

Sam was charismatic, good with women, and at the age of 24 had just got out of prison. He had broad shoulders, a loud mouth, and a "mad dog" glare that could make a grown man whimper. I not only looked up to Sam, I wanted to emulate him. When he called, I usually came running.

I broke the news to Christina of my sudden change of plans. "You're just gonna leave me here?" she asked sadly, clinging to me tighter, the disappointment in her voice palpable. Insensitive to her hurt feelings, I tried to charm my way out of the uncomfortable exchange. "I'll be back soon, I promise," I said as I broke our embrace and gave her a reassuring smile.

Sprinting back to my house, I changed into club attire. Slacks, dress shirt, and a black, serrated knife in my pocket. At 17 years old, clubbing was my unlawful indulgence. Lying about my age and hanging out with older crowds made me feel important. I could be whoever I wanted in the fluorescent ambiance of bouncer-guarded doors and velvet ropes, a baby-faced mystery as I stumbled between shadowed booths and lacquered tables. Checking out my outfit with approval, I flew out the door towards Karnak.

When I arrived a few minutes later, Sam was outside the nightclub waiting for me. "What the fuck took you so long?" he said with a slightly irritated slur. Locking his arm around my neck in a playful embrace, he flashed his drunken smile, "Come on, let's go in!"

Inside, a few homegirls waited for us at a small round table. A fruit platter, shot glasses, and a half-empty Crown Royal bottle haphazardly decorated the varnished marble.

"Hey cutie!" the girls squealed, greeting me with hugs and kisses.

I tried standing a little taller, puffing my chest and flexing my arms. They oozed sexuality in their tight jeans and skimpy tops. However, they were a couple years older than me and always treated me like a little kid. My flirtatious advances were usually met with a pinch of my cheeks and "If only you were a little older..." *I'm a grown ass man,* I thought, more disappointed than anything else.

After a few shots of the liquor, I crowned myself king of the dance floor. It never took much to get me going, the liquid napalm blasting away my inhibitions. E40's "Tell Me When To Go" and 50 Cent's "Disco Inferno" blared from the speakers as I danced sloppily, grinding my pelvis against the ladies. Disco lights, fog machines, and the deep bass rumbled in my chest, adding to the animalistic fervor.

As I returned to our table, the vibration of my phone buzzed against my thigh. Through the haze of cigarette smoke, Christina's name flashed on the screen. I went outside to escape the noise. "When are you coming back?" she pleaded, her voice was muffled by the ringing in my ears.

Before I could answer, I saw the fast movement of a scuffle in my peripheral vision. Squinting to take a closer look, I recognized Sam in the middle of the street fighting two strangers. *Who the fuck?!*

I told Christina I'd call her back. Rushing to join the skirmish, I dug into my pocket and withdrew my knife. With a swift snap of the wrist, it slapped open with a loud crack. Immediately, our opponents fled from the fight like cockroaches from light. I pursued one of them and swung violently, plunging my blade into his arm.

Drunk and oblivious of my surroundings, I was unaware that police officers were watching the whole crime unfold. "Drop the knife!" they screamed, guns drawn.

Scared and in a pathetic attempt to save myself, I tossed my bloody blade into some bushes. They quickly recovered it and restrained me in cuffs. As I was shoved against the police car, the person that I had knifed maneuvered around the police officers and struck me with his leaking arm. His slimy blood smeared across my face.

We finally arrive at Central Juvenile Hall. Driving into the cul-de-sac, we park in front of a pasty green door. It's my first time incarcerated, and it feels more like bees than butterflies in the pit of my stomach. The alcohol buzz wearing off adds to the nest of my growing problems.

The police officers take me out of the car and walk me on wobbly legs into a processing cell. Two teenagers, no more than 14 or 15 years old, mop and sweep the hallway. Dressed in identical charcoal grey pants, white shirts, and latex gloves, they give me a quizzical look. It's probably not every day they see a kid dressed in a dress shirt and slacks come through their halls. A large Hispanic staff member, Mr. Esparza, comes in and hands me a bundle of clothes and a brown paper bag. "Hurry up and change. Throw your street clothes in here."

After changing into the garb of the drones, I hand the bag back to my overseer. I am taken to a small medical office where a nurse checks my vitals. As she asks a few medical questions, I notice a young girl sitting across the room dressed in similar attire, rubbing her baby bump. She couldn't be more than 14 years old. I watch her in sympathy as she cradles her protruding stomach, her dangling feet swinging back and forth like a child on a swing.

Mr. Esparza escorts me across a large green field towards several housing buildings. As I get closer, the pounding in my chest is echoed by the pounding of a hundred fists against thick glass windows. Pale faces crowd the dark windows as they twist their fingers into gang signs and mouth the name of their neighborhoods. "Don't worry, they're just window bangers," Mr. Esparza smirks and scoffs.

I approach the building with the letters "K, L" and "M, N" painted on its corners. Walking up a flight of stairs, I enter a dayroom area and go into an office where a senior staff gives me a spill about the "do's" and "don'ts" and assigns me to "M" unit. On the other side of the office is a large bathroom with four showerheads and four toilet stalls. There are no curtains or doors, providing a clear view of the inmates using the facilities. A guy sitting on the toilet, pants around his ankles, stares me down and throws up his gang sign. *Are you kidding me? Banging on me while taking a shit?*

I enter the recreational room where long tables extend out of the walls. Each table is marked by a NFL team logo and is busy with activity. A few people huddle in conversation, some play Uno, and a few scribble Old English letters on what looks like their homework. Feeling out of place like a kid at a new school, I find a seat at the closest table. A few people approach and ask me what gang I am from. I tell them with as much bravado as I can muster as they go back to their cards and coloring books, uninterested by my answers.

A skinny African-American kid sits next to me, introducing himself as "S.B." His childish exuberance is unthreatening and calms my nerves. He nods his head towards the last table with the huddled group of people.

"You're prolly gonna go in the cell with Sleepy. It's the only cell open."

He points out Sleepy as I make eye contact with a short, slightly chubby, Hispanic kid. He gives me a hard look and goes back to his conversation. By his furrowed expression, I anticipate a future conflict. S.B. continues to tell me some ground rules and expectations. "If you have an enemy in here, you gotta fight him", he says. He then shines a youthful smile and tells me about his goals for when he gets out. "I'm gonna make it big as a rapper!"

He snaps his fingers and beats on his chest like a drum. His freestyle is jammed with gang slangs and misogynistic slurs, then he transitions into a familiar 2Pac hook, "WHEN I GET FREE! MUTHA-FUCKAS BETTA WATCH THEY ASS! SOON AS I GET FREE IMA CLOCK SOME CASH!"

A few people join his impromptu cypher and soon four guys are rapping, "WHEN I GET FREE! MUTHA-FUCKAS BETTA WATCH THEY ASS!" I laugh along, the tension leaving my body as we bang on the table in a synchronized rhythm.

After dinner, it's movie time on an old box television in front of several rows of plastic lawn chairs. Excited voices fill the room as I find a seat in the front row next to S.B. "Let's watch *Fast and the Furious*!" one inmate yells. "Fuck that, lets watch *Menace II Society*!" another shouts. After everyone settles in, the sound of high pitch exhaust pipes and engines roar out of the Sony relic. About 10 minutes into the movie, the abrupt scraping of plastic chairs followed by loud slaps of fists cracking cheekbones revs my heart rate. I turn to see two kids swinging fast and furiously as kids around them scatter.

Staff members rush in screaming "O.C. Warning!" filling the small room with pepper spray. They tackle the combatants to the floor, twisting and turning arms. The rest of the kids lie down on the floor, ducking for cover like an earthquake drill. One of the fighters is crying with snot and drool dribbling down his face. "Fuck you! Owww! It burns! Fuck you!" he screams as he is cuffed and taken away.

Everyone is coughing, the spray burns our throats, noses and eyes, suffocating us. I use my shirt as a makeshift gas mask to no avail. After the two perpetrators are escorted out, we are directed back to our rooms. *So...(cough) much for...(choking) movie night.*

I find my assigned room. Sleepy is standing in front of the door as he talks about the fight with his neighbor. He glares at me from the corner of his eye, fist balled, gauging my distance like a spaghetti western showdown. *One... Two...* The tension breaks as a staff member shouts for everyone to get ready to enter their rooms. Sleepy proceeds to take off his pants and shoes and sets them neatly in front of the door. He slips his legs into the sleeves of his sweater, improvising a pair of pants. I watch everyone else do the same and follow suit.

In the room, we break the ice and share a little bit about each other. I find out that we live pretty close, he is in for grand theft auto, and has a pregnant girlfriend. He has been here for the past 30 days and hopes that at his next court hearing he will be released. He offers me a pencil and paper in case I want to write someone. I politely decline. Lying on his stomach, tongue sticking out of the corner of his mouth in deep focus, he begins writing to his girlfriend. "Dear Chaparrita," flows from his head through his lead in long fancy script.

Visions of my mother project onto the back of my eyelids as I try to fall asleep. I imagine her sitting on my cold bed, her worried eyes filling with tears and disappointment. Since I moved in with her, she has become adept to the workings of probation offices and courthouses. The more I think about her, the harder it is to hold back tears. I shake my head, trying to think about something else.

My thoughts turn to Sam. Sitting cuffed in the back of the police car, he worried that violating his parole would send him back to prison. "Don't trip Sam, I'm gonna tell the cops I did it," I said confidently, masking my fear behind a brave veneer. I wanted to show him that I wasn't afraid, that I was tough. I grit my teeth in determination. *I did what I had to do.*

My jaw relaxes and my heart flutters as Christina's face floats into my head. She is beautiful as she twirls and dazzles in my mind. I think about our late-night phone calls, her soft voice egging me on to talk for a little while longer. My chest tightens as I think about her standing alone in that parking lot, waiting for someone who wasn't coming. My heart squeezes every ounce of regret I have left. As the exhaustion of the day overcomes me, lingering thoughts of my ballerina follow me into my dreams. *Christina...Wait for me...*

***

When the weekend rolls around, I anxiously wait on a green bench watching families walk in and hug their delinquent sons. It's visiting day. Searching the crowded line of people, I see my mother stunted by the overweight woman in front of her. My mother's appearance is gaunt and fatigued. The stress of her son in Juvenile Hall is obviously taking a toll. As she approaches me, my heart pounds in my chest and ears. I can no longer hold back my tears. We hug in a powerful embrace as we cry on one another's shoulders. After a minute, she examines me at arm's length, questioning me about my health and diet like a doctor. She runs her fingers through my short hair before cradling my face in her hands. She tries to hide her shock when I tell her what I have done as shame and regret compel my profuse apologies.

When visiting hours end, mothers and fathers give their sons parting words backed by embraces. My mom grips my hands tightly and looks intently into my eyes. "Justin, promise me you will stop living the way you have been, promise me that you will be good." Her eyes gloss on the verge of tears as she begs me to obey her.

"I promise Mom, I promise."

***

After a couple of weeks, about a dozen of us, each connected through crime and a single handcuff attached to a long chain, walk across the now familiar recreational field to the courthouse. It's judgment day.

We walk single file into a room with rows of long wooden pews. Sliding clumsily onto the benches, I duck under my chain as I reposition my cuff. I feel like I am in a church, waiting for some divine message, only this congregation could care less about repentance.

Court papers are handed out with charges and recommended sentences. I hear a fretful voice whine that he's looking at six months. I am handed my paper and read it in disbelief. Assault with a deadly weapon, recommended sentence, 2-4 years. I quickly do the math in my head and my heart drops as I think selfish thoughts about what I will miss, *my 18th birthday... Christina will leave... My friends will forget me... I pray desperately for salvation. God, please get me out of this, I promise I will be good, I will go to church every Sunday!* I sit in growing anguish as I mumble prayers and empty promises.

I watch the revolving door of inmates go in and out of the courtroom, each one's mask of toughness returning with cracks frosm the judge's gavel. It's my turn, and I walk in with a dismal disposition. A lawyer, Mr. Chang, greets me. He wears gold-rimmed glasses and has dark black hair with slivers of silver slipping in and out of his scalp.

He tells me that my mom hired him and that he has good news, "You'll be getting out tomorrow with two months house arrest."

I cannot believe it! Gratitude and relief replace my despair as my heart fills to bursting on the way back to my housing unit. Everyone greets me with shoulder bump hugs, congratulating me as if I've done something impossible.

I lie on my bunk for my last night in Juvenile Hall. I talk with Sleepy for a while and wish him luck with his case and his baby. We got close these past weeks as we cracked jokes and traded war stories. Behind his hardened demeanor, he has a soft, gentle side. He's just a kid, terrified of being a father as he wrote long love letters to his "Chaparrita". I think about Sam and my friends, our reunion to be celebrated with alcohol and partying. I think about all the stories I will tell them as I bask in the glory of my first stint.

I squeeze my pillow tightly as Christina prances back into my mind. My heart races as I imagine holding her and the sweet smell of her shampooed hair. Promises to God and my mom become brittle recollections I consciously try to avoid. There is too much to do, to make up for lost time, butterflies tickling inside for tomorrow's adventures. As the excitement consumes me, I close my eyes to welcome dreams of gangsters and nightclubs when a familiar 2Pac song enters my mind...*when I get free, mutha-fuckas betta watch they ass...*

The Mask of Wacko

Bryant Salas

When I was 16, the girl who was the existence of my whole being broke up with me and it really hurt. I felt rejected and lost. I had alienated myself from pretty much everyone at school because I just wanted to spend all my time with her. As she pulled away from me and I saw her carrying on with her friends as if our break up didn't effect her at all, I felt worthless and unimportant. I didn't know how to move on. I had nothing else. I felt like I didn't fit in anywhere else. So I started ditching school and cutting myself on my wrist with a razor. I can remember the inspiration coming from a familiar song by Eminem that said, "Sometimes I even cut myself to see how much it bleeds, it's like adrenaline, the pain is such a sudden rush for me." The physical pain took away from the inner turmoil I was going through.

My dad started getting on my case because he found out I wasn't going to school. One day he came into my room and saw it was a mess. I had thrown stuff around in a fit of anger. He started putting me down. In a cry for help, I showed him my wrist and told him he didn't know me or care. He responded by telling me to stop being a little "B" - if I was going to do it, to just do it. That hurt me so much. I had exposed my shame to my dad and he had in essence told me to kill myself. He didn't care about me. That is what I believed.

I started to hang out with my older brother and his friend and smoked crystal meth for the first time with them. I felt all alone, and I just wanted so bad to do something besides feel like I was a loner. And I wanted to forget all about my heartbreak. I got sprung on meth. It became a habit quick. I wasn't thinking about my ex when I was out with my brother and his friends and we were getting high. I wasn't thinking about anything except getting high. I began stealing stuff from my own house to support this habit. It caused more problems between my dad and me because his tools started going missing. When I had nothing else of value to pawn in my house, I started to rob houses to support my habit and to show my brother that I could contribute, too.

Around this time, I had a falling out with my crew. My friend asked me to hold his gun and the neighbor from across the street jacked it. The way it happened was I showed it to him while we were smoking dope, he chambered a round, and then walked off with it. I was afraid to try to stop him because I didn't want it to go off by accident. His mom came across the street and said that her cousin (who was a gang member) needed to use it. I knew right then that I wasn't getting it back. I felt like such an idiot and afraid of what I was going to tell my friend who trusted me to hold it. I was ashamed of what happened, so I didn't tell him the truth. Instead, I said I was chased by the cops and tossed it in the bushes. I even went to where I "threw it" with a rake and attempted to retrieve it. He told me I was full of it and pointed out that the dope was messing me up. He made it clear that I was going to pay for it one way or another.

I avoided him as much as possible after that. I stayed inside and wouldn't even go to the door, until one day he showed up with a bunch of guys from the crew and said that I was gonna be jumped out. I felt like there was nowhere else to go. I went outside and fought this one guy whose mission it was to fight me, so he could take my place in the crew. We fought until my dad came outside and watched from the doorway. I remember seeing him and thinking, *why isn't he helping me or stopping this?* The fight stopped when my friend saw my dad and said that's it. When it was over I heard my friend say, "At least he got down," and that made me feel good. It was freeing. I wasn't so ashamed anymore. I didn't have to hide from him anymore.

I kept smoking meth with my brother and the guys from across the street until one day when this guy who I presumed to be a gang member (the same guy that ended up with the gun) came to my door threatening to "cause mayhem" if he did not get his wallet back. He thought my brother, who had been across the street smoking dope with him, had stolen it. My brother denied taking it and left me and my little sister to fend for ourselves. I remember being angry that my brother had left us there like a coward. My little sister was hysterical because she had heard the threats of violence from this person at the door. Her fear fed into mine, so I told her to go to her room and call my mom.

I went and grabbed a machete I had in my room and waited. The longer I waited, the more scared I became. I felt like I was really going to have to kill this guy because I thought my brother was lying and I believed this guy was fully capable of doing what he said he would. He was a gang member and, in my mind, that's what gang members did. I eventually got so I scared I just called the police. I told them that a drugged-up gang member from across the street, who was most likely armed, had come to our house and threatened us with mayhem. I told them we needed help but to please not come to our house because I didn't want the guy to know I called. They showed up and got him. I found out later that he had found his wallet after all. But it was too late. It was done. I felt so ashamed. I felt like the coward now. Growing up I was taught you don't snitch, and that was exactly what I had done. I felt weak. I was also scared. I didn't want anyone to know I was the one who had called the police. I even insinuated to others that my mom had called. I felt like I had a whole other secret that I had to hide now. I distanced myself from everyone in that scene. I just felt uneasy about the whole thing.

Not long after this incident my brother got arrested for burglary. I remember going to visit him at the substation with my mom. It really hurt me deep in my chest seeing him behind that glass, afraid and vulnerable, with seven stiches across his brow from a police officer's boot. I felt for him. I saw someone who needed help and was scared but was trying not to show it. I related to that. He was sentenced to a year. I remember that felt like a lifetime to me.

My relationship with my dad was already strained but when my brother went to prison, whatever anger and contempt he felt towards us was doubled on me. He would get on my case constantly, until he just kicked me out. He even nailed the windows shut so I couldn't get inside when no one was there. This made me feel completely rejected and unwanted. This compounded the feeling that my dad didn't care about me.

I started to stay at my cousin's house again. He was on this music-making trip. He had got a beat machine and would make beats and I would write lyrics to them. We'd do that, and just smoke weed and hang out. The good thing was that he didn't smoke meth so I let that go for a bit. His older brother, my cousin, started coming through to hang out with us. He was fresh out of prison. I didn't know him well because he was away all the time, either in the streets or prison. Nevertheless, what I did know about him made me look up to him. He was a gangster, he was tatted up, and he just had this 'F___ it" confidence that I wanted so badly. I felt this sense of security when I was with him. He showed me attention and he made me feel at home, like he liked having me around. Because I had been kicked out by my dad, I ate it up.

He started to invite me to hang out with him and his homies. I felt special because he wouldn't even take his little brother to go kick it. So I started hanging out with them. We'd smoke weed and drink. I got introduced and sprung on primos, which is weed sprinkled with rock cocaine and rolled in a blunt. Now that I was sprung on rock, I wasn't just going over for the acceptance from my cousin and his friends. I was really looking forward to smoking rock. I really started to feel like I was a part of these guys. I felt accepted there.

One day while out with my cousin we went to this girl's house that he knew. I went down the street from there to another girl's house. While I was talking to this girl, my cousin came up and said there was a guy down the street saying that he saw me crying over at my ex-girlfriend's house. I immediately got defensive and denied it ever happened. I went to where this guy was at to confront him. I got aggressive with him and snatched him by his shirt. I told him to keep my name out off his mouth or I was going to whip his ass. He remained calm and collected because he was telling the truth. I was angry that this guy had seen me in a vulnerable state and felt like he was making me look weak. I contemplated taking his car but thought better. Instead, I let his shirt go at the plea of the girl who I knew and liked. I turned and walked away feeling embarrassed and angry that this guy had this thing on me. So I turned on my heel and threw up the gang sign for Happy Town at him for the first time ever. And I decided right then and there that I had to redeem myself and the gang was gonna be how. I needed to make a new name for myself.

The next time I went to hang out with my cousin and "the homies", the usuals were there, but there was a different feel. They had plans to jump me and another guy in that day. I was asked first and I was afraid. I knew what it entailed to be a gang member because another cousin of mine, who was an ex-gang member himself, told me that I was gonna be made into a murderer if I went down this path. My whole tough guy role was a cover up for the insecurity and powerlessness I felt, so when asked I said, "I'm not sure I'm ready for that." They proceeded to ask the other guy and he responded, with no hesitation, "Put me on." And they did. After he was jumped in and the handshakes and hugs were given, we left. On the way out the ally, I could see the disappointment in my cousin's eyes. I asked him if I had let him down. He said, "Yes, you did." It really hurt. I felt that familiar feeling of being worthless, unaccepted, and good for nothing. All the things my dad made sure to let me know I was.

As we went back to the house to hang out and smoke to celebrate the new recruit, it just didn't feel the same. I felt like an outsider, like I didn't belong. The same way I felt at home. Before leaving, they asked me one more time if I wanted to be from the hood. They said, "It's now or never." I said okay, and I got jumped in by my cousin and two other people. I fought back with everything I had to prove that I was worthy, strong enough, and not afraid. When it was done, I was embraced the same as the other guy. Hugs and smiles all around. We even smoked a blunt over it, and this time it felt right. I didn't feel like I was an outsider anymore and my cousin was proud of me.

I was there every day after getting jumped in. We would smoke, drink, vandalize the walls with spray paint, and kick it with girls. It wasn't long before I would participate in my first act of gun violence. One day while patrolling the neighborhood, we passed a party with people spilled out onto the sidewalk. As we passed, everyone on the sidewalk ducked except for one defiant individual. We didn't appreciate that, so we went and grabbed a gun. As we pulled over down the street from the party, I was handed a .38 special, a bandana, and a beanie, and told to take care of him.

I got out of the car and made my way down the street, taking cover five cars down from where this group was. They couldn't see me, so I knelt and took aim at this guy. In that moment, I remembered what a teacher in high school once told me about it being hard to shoot a real gun. I took cover behind the car again. I didn't want to shoot someone else by accident, but I knew the homies were waiting on me and they would know if I didn't shoot. I didn't want them to think I was scared, so I stood in the middle of the street, yelled, Happy Town!" and fired two shots into a parked car. I ran back and we sped off. They asked if I got him, and I lied, saying, "I think so, but I'm not sure. It was dark and everyone got down." I was congratulated, and I soaked it in. I felt powerful making everyone react in that way. After that day, I always wanted to hold the gun when we were out. It gave me a sense of confidence. I liked having the upper hand on others.

As my reputation went up, I saw it came with a lot of perks. I had a number of girls who were into me just because I was a gang member. As an insecure individual, I really appreciated that I was desired and that I didn't have to pursue them, because they pursued me. My ex-girlfriend even came back into my life. I felt as if I had everything I wanted: power, money, women and respect.

I even got what I perceived to be respect from my dad. One night, when only my dad and I were home, he came into my room drunk and looking to pick a fight. This time was different because he was egging me on to hit him, so it could have become physical. He called me every name in the book while blocking my exit through the front door. And all I could think was, *who does he think he is getting at me like this? He doesn't know who I am and what I'm capable of.* Eventually he moved, and I exploded out the door and fired a shot from my .25 hand gun. I wanted him to know that I could have shut him up if I wanted to, that I wasn't weak but powerful and not to be taken lightly. He opened the door and threatened to call the police, so I ran. But I had nowhere to go, so I just circled the block.

I heard him calling my name as I got close to the house. It was as if he had completely sobered up. He told me to go to my room, that he'd leave me alone, and that he hadn't called the cops. I went inside confused that he had broken down. I came to the conclusion that he got my point loud and clear. He would still be on my case about what I was going to do with my life, but not like that night. I remember shutting him down one day by saying, "what does it matter what I do? I am going to be in jail for life anyway."

My life had become a big performance. I just wanted to feel strong and accepted and I was willing to do anything and hurt anyone to feel that. I reinforced my life with raps about the gang lifestyle and put more pressure on myself to be a real gangster. I proved myself by fighting and banging on anyone who looked my way. This image was challenged one day when I was kicking it with some girls and the homies. One of the homies (who I felt thought I was full of it) told me to tell a war story in front of everyone. I had nothing, and I was embarrassed and felt belittled and weak. I knew I had to do something to prove myself. I got that chance not long after. While hanging out in the neighborhood, this same guy who put me on the spot ran up to me and asked if I had a gun because he had just been banged on. I said yes, and he asked me to give it to him. I said, "No, I'll take care of it." And we jumped in the car to look for this guy.

When we found him, I jumped out, ran up to his window and pulled the trigger 6 times. The gun didn't fire. I was confused. I jumped back in the car and we sped off. They asked what happened and I said I don't know. I opened the cylinder of the .32 revolver even more confused because every bullet had been hammered. That story went around just because of how odd it was. And my reputation went around with it. I got respect from the guy who was implying I wasn't with the business and my name went around. Again, I soaked it in.

I started a part time job in pest control with my cousin. We'd spend our mornings working and afterward I'd get dropped off in the hood. I was involved in everything. I was given dope by my homie, so I could make some extra money, and it made me feel like I was trusted. They even liked the music I was making. In my mind, they only liked it because I was living everything I was talking about. I felt validated, but it was a lot of pressure.

On February 23rd, 2007, this pressure would rear its ugly head and leave an everlasting impact. It started just like any other day. I woke up and went to work with my cousin. I actually didn't go to the hood as usual but went back to Rancho Cucamonga with my cousin. The evening came around he decided to go to the movies with his girlfriend. He invited me, but I didn't want to be a third wheel with them and I didn't care for her much either. I encouraged him to go and he did, but I felt left out and abandoned by him. It didn't take long for me to get bored and restless. My other cousin came by looking to get some weed. Right away, I told him we could get it in the hood. I knew there wasn't any, but I just wanted to go, so we did. When we showed up, there were the usual guys there. They were talking about checking someone, so I went with three other guys and we spray-painted "Happy Town" on this guy's garage. We returned as my cousins were getting ready to leave. My cousin said, "Let's go, they don't have any bud," but I didn't want to be alone at my cousin's house, so I said I was staying. He asked me if I was sure in a tone that expressed concern. I said "Yeah, I'll be alright."

We decided to get some beer so we could go kick it. We pulled into a shopping center where the beer was cheaper, according to my homie. As we were about to park the car, I noticed a group of guys to my right, exiting their cars and walking in the direction of the Denny's. I instantly started to mad dog them from my seat in the back of the car. I locked eyes with one guy who was wearing a "wife-beater". I remember thinking, this guy is drunk. When he didn't back away from my stares but instead decided to walk up to my window, I took it as a challenge. I heard my homie driving tell me to wait, but I didn't. I thought, *how dare this guy not back down from me?*

I exited the care and asked this guy if he knew where he was at, implying that he was in my neighborhood. He responded, "You have a problem with Koreans?" Surrounded by this guy and his friends and fueled by my insecurities, my need to be seen as strong and unafraid, I responded, "This is Happy Town. I have a problem with everybody!" and punched him. I was instantly rushed by all these guys and met them head on. It was a free for all. I didn't see my friends get out the car, but I knew they would and they did. All four of us fought against at least ten or eleven guys. I was holding my own. I remember even going to help my youngest homie (who was fourteen at the time) from being stomped out. I got the guy off of him with a punch to the back of the head. As I looked up, I was punched in the face.

I locked in on this guy. As I approached him, I heard someone say, "He's got a knife!" I didn't know who said it, but I instantly looked around so as not to get stabbed. As I scoped out the scene, I realized the car had been pulled towards the exit. As soon as I saw the car, I realized the guys were jumping in it. I followed them and was the last one in. Someone in the car shouted, "Happy Town!" as we drove off. I was now seated behind the driver's seat, and as I looked back, I remember seeing the guy in the "wife-beater" doubled over, as if catching his breath.

We sped down the road filled with adrenaline and hooting and hollering about the fight. As we drove away, my friend driving asked me for a rag to wrap his hand because he had cut himself. When I asked him how he cut himself, he said, "The knife closed on me." I said, "What knife?" He replied, "I stabbed that mother F'er." Another other homie said, "Yeah me too." He handed back an oversized pocketknife and we proceeded to where we were gonna hang out. Later that night when I went to my cousin's house, I told him to turn on the news. Two people had been stabbed and one air lifted to the hospital. Kevin Fu died at the hospital that night from a single stab wound to his lower abdomen. His friend Christopher Cheng survived a stab wound to the back.

Chainfire of the Killing Fields

Thaisan Nguon

My family immigrated to America when I was a newborn. We fled the genocide that was ravaging our homeland of Cambodia. I was told that we were able to come to America through some sort of sponsorship program where an American family took our family under their tutelage to help us get acclimated to American culture. I recall living in two other states before we settled in California. The first place we called home was Joliet, Illinois and the second place we called home was Fortworth, Texas. My childhood memories from back then are too hazy to fully recall. It's probably because I was fairly young. The memories that I can recall happen to take place after I arrived in Long Beach, California in 1986.

I remember how excited I was to move to California. My Dad had promoted the move as a fun adventure that the whole family would enjoy. So I drew from him that energy of optimism. I recall looking forward to the first day of school. I had visions of making tons of friends and incorporating myself into my new school quite smoothly. To my dismay, that was not the case. My first day of school was marred with ridicule. I was made fun of by what seemed to be the whole school. In actuality it was just two separate groups of bullies, about a handful deep, respectively. One group was all Hispanics and the other group was all African-Americans. They both made fun of my ethnicity and I never felt so helpless and so small. I had never experienced racial prejudice before. My reaction to it was to retract into myself. I endured their taunts because I feared what would happen if I dared to stand up to them.

For my first and second grade school year, I attended two different schools and experienced the same racial indignation from my peers. By my third-grade year, I had had enough, so I started to push back. I mimicked the same hurtful behavior that worked so well to degrade my self-worth. When Hispanic or African-American kids pulled their eyes back to tighten them and said, "Ching chong, ching chong," I would respond in kind with my own racial slur. If they persisted, I would resort to violence. I got into many playground fights this way. By this time, violence had become an acceptable form of behavior for me.

When I was about 6 years old, my dad witnessed me being bullied and pushed around by a neighborhood kid. When he saw me get knocked down and proceed to walk back home again, he insisted on blocking the doorway. He told me I was not permitted to step into the house until I fought the kid who had pushed me down. So I did. Other Asian kids who were treated the way I was and felt the way I did about their own mistreatment began to fight back as well. Gradually we all began to gravitate towards one another and started to resemble a sort of quasi-Asian-gang for elementary school kids.

As all of this was going on in my school life, the home front wasn't treating me any better. I often felt abused and neglected. It seemed that I was being whooped by my mom every day for something or another. The justification for my beatings ranged from exhibiting an attitude towards household chores to playing with matches and almost burning down the house. I was somewhat of a mischievous kid. Every time I got whooped by my mom, it created a distance between us that made me feel that my dad loved me more. My dad was hardly around but when he was, he never hit me. As a matter of fact, he often came to my rescue whenever he was around to witness one of my whoopings. I saw my dad as my own personal hero because of that. And because of his noticeable absence in my childhood, all I did as a kid was wish that he was around more. He could do no wrong in my eyes. That was true until it wasn't anymore. He broke my sensitive little heart at a time when I needed to feel the love of a parent most.

When I was 8 years old, my dad kidnapped me. He woke me up in the middle of the night and asked me if I would like to go live with him and my Grandma. If so, we would have to leave immediately so my mom wouldn't find out. On the car ride out he told me that my second family would be coming with us. My second family consisted of my stepmother (a woman who my dad had been having an affair with since before I was born), my stepbrother (my stepmother's oldest son from her first marriage), and my half-brother (the love-child produced from their relationship). I had no problem with our potential blended household, so long as I was with my dad. The new family dynamic didn't bother me.

When we arrived at my grandma's in Massachusetts, I felt that something was off. I was told to go run along and play with the other kids while the grown-ups spoke. After all the grown-ups had their talk, my dad told us that we had to go. As I collected myself, he stopped and said that I would be staying with my grandma while he and my stepfamily went to another relative's house. I was confused because I thought we were all going to be together. I told him as much and reminded him of what he had said to me when we left home. His only response was that this is how it is going to have to be for the meantime. As he drove off, leaving me with my grandma, I recall feeling utterly sad and abandoned.

I felt like my dad didn't really care about me at all. Or if he did, he loved his other family more. Why else would he leave my family so easily then abandon me at my grandma's house? After that moment, the love and admiration I once carried for him slowly began to erode. Our relationship strained and whatever parental authority he held over me ceased to exist. I stayed with my grandma in Massachusetts for the rest of the school year. I returned to California, and to my mom, in the summer of '89. I wish I could say after my dad took me away from her for a year, that my mom held back on the whoopings, but no, she did not. She might have restrained herself that first year, but it was business as usual after that.

My experiences with my parents and with racism made me very self-conscious. I was insecure and had low self-esteem. I used aggression and violence to mask my insecurities because I didn't want to be seen as weak. A lot of my friends were the same way, aggressive and violent, that is. Like I said earlier, we gravitated towards one another due to the cruelties of racism and as we bonded over our feelings of injustice, we all decided to start up our own little crew. Soon, we grabbed the attention of a bigger and well-known Asian gang and eventually got incorporated into that gang. If I'm being honest, I was scared out of my mind to join a real gang. When I was a part of my crew, we just had each other's back and made sure one another did not suffer bullying and/or beat downs because of the way we looked. I knew that joining a gang was some next level shit. And I didn't think I was capable of doing the things that I heard gang members were supposed to do. Nevertheless, I joined a gang. There was an indescribable feeling of being loved and camaraderie in the gang. Plus, I didn't want my friends to think I didn't have their backs and I didn't want to look like I was scared. I was 13 years old when I joined.

The first time I ever got arrested was my first day of high school. I was 14 years old and I was arrested for possession of a butterfly knife on school grounds. The crazy thing about that was the knife was passed to me by my "Big Homie" when we saw that the school security was randomly patting people down as they entered school grounds. I had a feeling that the security staff saw the hand off but I didn't say anything because I didn't want to look like I was scared to hold a knife or get arrested. But I was both those things.

I recall praying that I not go to jail because being incarcerated was one of my top five fears. I was able to avoid jail time but that didn't mean I didn't suffer any consequences. Being arrested for a butterfly knife set me on a course where my education was stymied because I was banned from the public school system. My family suffered financially because my dad had to take off work just to take me to all those court dates and he was the primary earner in the household. As bad as I felt for the negative impact that my arrest caused for me and my family, I carried on like I was big and tough because of my arrest and acted like I didn't have a care in the world about it. I felt somewhat like a fraud for feeling scared and yet pretending as if I wasn't.

One of the scariest moments I experienced as a gang member was when I first got initiated in. A rival gang had chased me into a glass window store and I was able to find a hiding place between two workbenches. As I laid there, still as can be, I saw four guys walk in the store with weapons in their hands. One had a bat, another had a metal pipe, a third carried a knife, but the one that spooked me the most was the guy who had one hand in his pocket. The object in his pocked seemed to me to be a gun and my whole soul immediately started to pray for God to shroud me from their eyes. I was so scared to make a sound that I held my breath for fear of breathing too loud and bringing attention to my position. The incident underscored how dangerous serious gang banging was, but in my own mind, I still saw it as a bunch of bullies trying to push me around. In that sense, I became defiant.

My level of criminality gradually progressed as my time in the gang did. The gang life and crime went hand in hand. There always existed a sense of fear whenever I committed a crime, but I pushed through that fear because my want of being accepted was more powerful. This feeling of wanting to be accepted would lead to my demise. I would lean on it to ignore my moral compass and sense of right and wrong. I assaulted people, robbed people, and engaged in shootings with reckless abandonment. The more I partook in these activities, the further removed I became from my humanity. The further detached I became from my own humanity, the easier it became for me to devalue the humanity in others. This would lead me to be involved in a murder and attempted murder that would forever change the lives of many people. I might not have personally pulled the trigger that killed V.T. and shot S.M. in the head, but that fact makes no difference. I am just as responsible because of the irresponsible and reckless choices I made that day and throughout my entire life. This murder and attempted murder are my biggest regrets and they will forever weigh heavily on my heart and conscience.

Three Poems

George Sanchez[1]

Destroying the Property

The Pen
Didn't work
At first when
I tried to
Tag around my
Room.
Magically, it worked
And I tagged
On the bunk.
On the side.
I pressed the pen.
But it was very light.
Some spots, it didn't
Spread the ink.
So I'd position the
Tip
Of the
Pen a one way
and
it began to
Work magically.
Then on
the
center of
the
top bunk.

Where there
Aint a mat.
I started to
Tag up the hood again.
I added my details.
But I'd stop my
Work and check
The door if
Any staff were
Doing their room checks.
Not a staff.
I ran back.
Got on top of the
Stool.
Reached for the top
bunk and vandalized.
Destroyed state property.
Not resting my arms
On the side
Because the ink
might get my shirt
stained.

---

1 These poems have intentionally been left unedited in an effort to preserve and prioritize the voice of the author.

Kool-Aid Up and Down the Room

Walked up
My room.
Walked down
My room.
Not much space.
Any sudden
Movement
Outside.
I ran to
The
Door in the
Hopes
That I'll
Hold up
A staff to
Get
Me paper.
I'm done.
No more sheets
Of
Poetry
The only human to
Bring me
The second tool
To
Art and that paper
has disappeared.
There was
an incident in the
next door unit.
A Riote.

Could of been
My homies, against
The north.
Could of been
The north with the Bulldogs.
The staff are gone.
I mix the state
Kool-Aid
In
A plastic orange cup.
With a spork
I mix the Kool-Aid
perfectly.
I begin to
Drink
Its tasty but
It can be better
So I therefore
Rip open
A 3rd Kool-Aid
Packet and
Let it go in the cup
I didn't know
If what
Was already
In the water
Was orange flavor
Kool-Aid but
I mixed a lemon
Flavor Kool-Aid
Last. A lot more

Tasty
Walked up
my room.
Walked down
My room.
Drinking my orange
Cup with Kool-Aid.
I find
a staff
on the phone.
I began to bell out
For paper. But
He quickly disappears.
Into the office.
I curse, in Spanish
"puto."
More encounters
With them
But they disappear.
I start
Singing and rapping
With my
neighbor.
One staff said
"hold up."
Usual reply.
Another staff
Said
"when I got
a minute"

Drank Kool-Aid
Down my room
And up my room.
Rapped 2Pac songs.
Sang love songs.
Messed around
Disrespecting my
Neighbor and him
disrespecting me.
The short staff
In all black
Walks to my
Door
And
Squeezes the
Paper
Through.
Silence
Then…

Note Pad Doesn't Stay Forever

Running out of
Paper, once again.
Believe it or
Not, but I
Have to
Scavenge for
This stuff.
I had finally
Gotten the
Note pad I had
Bought from
My property.
I wrote
On it.
And its
About gone.
Wrote a
Good amount
Of
Poems from
The mind
And heart.
Spoke very
Vivid
About my
Past and
Present.
Usually its
The shouting
For paper
That displea
Ses me.

The staff are
Lazy and slow.
The wait for
Sheets of paper
Has me
Pasing my
Room. The pen
I was using.
The only pen.
Doesn't have ink.
Im on my mat
Thinking and get
a good idea for
a poem. Don't have
paper. Waiting
on a packet of
paper that the
staff wont
bring as quick
but slow. The
good topic
is becoming
less and
once I get
the paper.
The topic
Vanished
In thin space
In my brain.
I'll bring this
Up as well,
When

I do have
A lot of paper.
I don't
Got much
Inspiration to
Write. Boredom
Forces me to
Seek a
Sheet of paper
For
The purpose
of a poem.
But
I get real
Crazy.
And that
Craziness
Explodes to
Poems. It shocks
Me to go over
My poems.
Where did I get
This
Monster? or
Flower from?
The long drive
To reach
My poems
Are crazy. Well
Im a crazy
Person that
Likes

To talk,
In poetry
But
The note
Pad is
over
with.

Daisies

Justin S. Hong

My sister was around 8 years old when she wanted her ears pierced. As her older brother, I made this my job. I got an earring, numbed her ear with an ice cube, and told her on the count of three. She tightened her face anticipating the pain, and one ...two...three! A loud pop and a daisy shaped earring hung from her tiny ear. I pierced the other side and when she looked in the mirror, the smile on her face was enough to make me feel like the best big brother ever.

Fearing what my dad would say, I insisted she hide them with her hair until the holes were healed. Then, she could put her pretty earrings in on her way to school and take them off when she came home. Our elaborate plan made it as far as to the dinner table that night. My dad saw the earrings and abruptly ended the meal. He yelled and asked who did it for her. The answer was obvious as I sat there in silence, terrified of the beating I would get. I looked at her, seeing her wide eyes fill with fearful tears and uncertainty. *What do I do?* her eyes screamed. I sat there, my head down, unable to accept responsibility for what I had done.

He took us into our room and gave us one more chance to come clean. We both faked ignorance. I was ordered to look towards the wall. He started with my sister, spanking her as he demanded that she tell him who pierced her ears. As I listened to my sister sob and scream with each smack, my heart cracked with disgrace. *Stop hitting her!* my mind pleaded, as I masked my shame with helpless anger. I didn't say a word.

My turn came next and he ordered me to put out my hands. The yardstick let out a furious shriek as it crashed across my palms. My persistent silence continued to warrant more swings, but this time I felt I deserved it for what I put my sister through. As tears rolled down my face, I looked to my sister's heaving body as she sobbed in the corner, facing the wall. *I'm so sorry.* My heart broke.

Considering my role as "Best big brother ever", not being there for my sister that day is a regret I will always carry. It is memories like this that remind me to be a better person, to believe in the goodness of others, and to cherish my connections with my loved ones. Every time she comes to visit me in prison, or sends pictures of her in Paris or Shanghai, her beautiful and tending spirit captivates me. We would each take turns receiving beatings that day. She refused to give me up no matter how much my father accused me. While this memory picks at old scabs, it also fills my heart with love. I focus on her glee as she caressed the daisies that

81

hung from her lobes, those few joyous moments as she stood on a stool adoring herself in the medicine cabinet mirror. It is only one of the many special memories that would bring us closer together. The resilient bond of a brother and sister, forged in the furnace of fear and love. My sister—Elaine, my daisy.

Dear Brother

Elaine Hong

Dear brother,

I realize that this is yet another letter that will not reach you. At least, not anytime soon. This letter will not be sent to Pelican State Bay Prison, Crescent City, CA, 10 miles south of Oregon, where forlorn trees and lingering fogs extend as far as the eye can see, where gloomy grey clouds block out the sun's existence above a barren wasteland, where animals seem to outnumber people, where time seems to have no meaning or existence, and where you reside in your cold cell which you call home.

Instead, this letter will be sent to a setting quite the opposite: the desk of a college admissions office in the bustling city of New York, one of the largest metropolises in the world. This letter is going to be read by a stranger, a stranger who knows nothing of me, or you, or our past. But at least this letter will not be another that I'll write with heartfelt emotion, just to be crumpled up and throw in the trash. I will no longer hide. This is me, and I will be heard. This letter will be victorious, without tear marks blotting out the ink beyond legibility, or sharp bitter words clawing their way out to hurt you. This letter will not be written in vain.

I often think about how unfair life is, and sometimes I wish I could just quit. You were never there for me when I needed you the most. Those preteen years were horrible. I was picked on for my homemade clothes. I was chubby, with a face full of pimples, and too awkward to fit in. You weren't there to scare off the boys, those who courted me, those who bullied me. You missed all of my swim matches and band performances, and you never picked me up after school like all my other friends' brothers did.

I could never brag to my peers of a brother who went to a successful college, because you never did. Most people who know me don't know you exist. What happened? What happened to those days when you and I would find euphoria splashing each other in the pool, or spend hours chasing around the neighborhood critters just for the fun of it? What happened to those times when we'd find sweet satisfaction jumping up and down on our twin sized beds, dancing our butts off to old-school Korean pop songs? Or those times we'd stage fashion shows in the snug confines of our room, pretending to play store and auction off our few articles of clothing? You'd dress me up so ridiculously, but I didn't care. I'm even sad to say I'm nostalgic for those times when you were far from nice to me, including that one summer when we lived in Stockton and you super glued my fingers together while I was sleeping. I woke up crying, and there were you in the corner, gasping for breath, tears streaming down your face, dying of laughter. I wonder what happened...

I remember that one Thanksgiving when you snuck out of the house against dad's orders and rode your bike all the way to KFC to provide me and grandma with a Thanksgiving dinner. It made me cry. Hard. You were only 13 or 14 at the time. We had both gotten in big trouble by dad earlier that day, I can't even remember what for, and were told that we wouldn't be having dinner, even on Thanksgiving Day. And still, you snuck out to make sure I could experience Thanksgiving. You risked getting beat up, yelled at, and punished all night, for me. Even dad was so taken aback, he retreated from his room to help grandma unpack and plate dinner. And we ate together, in fragile, awkward silence, but in peace. I will never forget. Your face looked so full of pride and mischief, your eyes were literally twinkling as you came back home with two white plastic bags dangling from each of your bike's handlebars, brimming with delicious fried chicken. It wasn't an elaborate turkey dinner, but it was, and always will be, the best Thanksgiving of my life. I will never forget it.

What happened? Life happened. You went your way and I went mine. The way you chose to live didn't match up to the standards dad had for you, and you were soon out of the house to live with mom in the faraway city of Los Angeles. I was stuck back home in the city of La Palma, which claimed two square miles of boring wasteland. I've missed you. It seems like we haven't had a real relationship since that terrible day you were forced out of the house in your whisper thin white t-shirt and hand me down shoes, holes and all. It seems like we haven't reconnected personally since that night I sat sobbing on the floor, while Dad told me to tell you goodbye for the last time. I still remember how much it hurt, I couldn't possibly cry harder if I wanted to. It all seems so long ago.

It's already been seven years, and I'm applying to college. I'm no longer that kid sister you had that worshiped your every move and vowed to hate dad for taking you and mom away from me. I've grown up. What happened to you is horrible, what happened to me was horrible. But what if things happened differently? You might still be out there, dealing drugs, making bad decisions, forgetting about me and your life back in La Palma.

I might still be angry and bitter at the world, determined to make everyone's life a living hell because I felt mine was. Maybe life isn't so unfair after all. I still have you, and you still have me. We both have lives that have found ways to use and abuse us, but at least we are still here, breathing, existing. I'm glad I still have you, even though you and I are more than 300 miles apart. Hopefully, if I find some luck in this game called life, I'll be heading more than 3,000 miles away to pursue my education. It scares me, but I know I'll be okay, because I already have everything I need, and I've already learned everything I need to in life.

Like you always say, you don't have a weak sister, and you never will, I promise you that. I love you brother, and I hope that somewhere, sometime in life, we will be reunited.

Until then, all my love,

Elaine

Smith Family Reunion

David Smith

My father killed my mother when I was 6 years old. He did it right in front of me, in front of all of us kids. My twin sisters, Denise and Debra, were 11. My brothers, Ronald and Gary, were 13 and 9.

What I remember most about my mother is her pretty swollen face from the beatings my father always gave her. Bruises and blood. It seemed like she was always cleaning blood off her face. I still miss her. I still love her, all 5 foot 4 inches, 110 ten pounds of her petite self, my dearly departed mother, Margret Smith.

I'm told she was a sales representative, I don't know for what company. I know she made the mistake of falling in love with a steel worker named Aubrey E. Smith. He was my father. He was 6 foot 3 inches, 240 pounds, and what he loved was to get drunk. I'm told he was jealous man, which makes sense, considering what he said to mama right before he killed her.

He'd start drinking and start accusing mama of being a bad woman. He used to throw her down on the floor and start choking her out and pounding her face with his fists. My brothers and sisters and I would scream for him to stop, screaming and crying, "Daddy, stop! Please stop!" But daddy wouldn't stop until after she was passed out. He'd keep punching her face even when she wasn't moving. Us kids would hold her, crying and begging her to wake up. Please wake up. We'd tell her we loved her and promised to be good. We always thought, "This time she's dead." When she'd finally wake up we'd all hold each other and cry.

The day came when she took us kids and fled. We moved from friends' and relatives' homes, house to house, on the run from my father. Eventually, he moved out of our house, so we could move back home. I was sad and confused when my father moved out. Part of me was happy and part of me felt bad for feeling happy. I still loved my father and I missed him.

On October 3, 1970, my dad was coming over to pick up us kids for the day. I was excited, I hadn't seen him in weeks. We were all up early, dressed and ready to go. The twins had on their pink dresses - they always wore dresses and their dresses always matched. My brothers and I wore Tough Skin jeans and striped tee shirts. Mommy was still in bed when daddy came in the house with a big beige canister. "Where's your mama? I wanna show her what I got."

We all followed him into the bedroom. Gary hopped in the bed and laid next to mommy. We all gathered around, excited to see what daddy brought. He stood at the foot of the bed, opened the canister and took out a bag of beans and a bag of rice. "And I brought this just for you, baby," he told my mother as he pulled a .38 Special out of the canister, "You cheatin', lying whore!" He shot my mother twice in the face and four times in her chest. Six quick shots that blasted our ears and exploded into my mother's body.

Her last words were, "Aubrey, please, no." She died the same way she lived when my father was around – terrified.

The twins grabbed my hands we took off running out of the house, crying our faces off.

We buried my mother at Lincoln Memorial Park Cemetery, Section P.39/ Lot #1. She was born on July 17, 1937. She died when she was 33.

My dad surrendered without incident when the LAPD arrived. He was convicted of murder and sentenced to 7 years to life.

Us kids moved in with our grandparents. They lived in a house just three blocks away, in our South Central neighborhood. They took care of us, gave us food and shelter and clothes and toys. We were taught morals and values, and we better had behaved.

We called our grandpa, Big Dad. He was a kind man who was a workaholic. Grandma, Big Mama, was from a military background. My mother had been her only child. She hated my father, and she sure hated me. I looked like my dad, and the older I got, the more I looked like him. My grandmother used to say to me, "You look just like that devil."

Big Mama was tough and strict and mean-tempered. Corporal punishment was issued without restraint. She always threw it in our faces that it was she who kept us all together, when she could have just let us, "Get lost in the system." My twin sisters both got pregnant at the age of 15 or 16 – just so they could get away from Big Mama.

Big Mama's favorite saying, right before she'd haul off and smack me in the face, was, "You look just like your ignorant ass dad!"

She took to beating me with a broom stick, if it was handy when she got the urge. If we were in the bedroom, she'd grab a coat hanger and start whacking my body, though most of the hits landed on my arms as I blocked my face. She loved to cut branches off the tree in the yard – called them switches – and whip me raw. She was always so angry, she must have been in a lot of pain, losing her daughter so tragically (I've since forgiven her). But I'd had enough by the time I was 13. I ran away and started living in the streets.

Everybody had a story. So many stories of hurt and pain. Nothing special about mine, it just happens to be mine.

American Gangster
Tyson Atlas

"Tyson, I have no choice but to sentence you to LIFE WITHOUT THE POSSIBILITY OF PAROLE!"

Those were the words that left my mother screaming with tears pouring down her face. The judge had just sentenced my father to 25 years to life and my teenage mind couldn't grasp the difference between our sentences.

My focus shifted and like a deer caught in headlights, I looked to my crying mother wondering if this would be the last time I would see her in person. Having just been convicted of assault on a peace officer, I highly doubted that the prison system would allow her to visit me with her newfound record.

Young, self-centered, with a gangster mentality, I never thought about the other woman in that room, with tears staining her face: the mother who also lost a teenage son yet had no chance of ever seeing him again on this side of eternity. Silent as a church house mouse, I sat there with tears streaming from the corners of my eyes.

I then looked toward the first pew of that courthouse. That's when I saw her, a youthful yet seasoned dark-skinned sister, whose age was only seen in the edges of her eyes. The grandmother of Gregory Smith had just spoken with strength and power to my father. It was the hurt and pain in her voice that caught my attention. As they moved us out of that courtroom, shackled and cuffed, I found myself in deep thought, contemplating something she said to my father.

"You have also killed your own son!"

I'm alive, I thought momentarily.

As we entered the holding cell, reality rapidly set in as my father jokingly said, "You gone have a few sock babies, but we gone be alright."

I only chuckled because of his humorous tone. Truth was that as those bars slammed shut, my body shuttered thinking of that cage as my coffin.

Soon we were escorted to the transport van. With shackles on our feet, I followed my father taking baby steps. I looked up towards the dark sky and thought,

Is this the last time I will see my father?

My thoughts were interrupted when the transport officer asked me, "Do you want to hear that new Jay-Z album: American Gangster?"

This officer had been transporting us all throughout our trial and we had become acquainted. While most officers treated us indifferently, he was kind and in some ways understood us. He often tried to lighten the mood with music and conversation.

"Today we will take the long way back," he said in his usual smooth tone.

As we passed by a familiar skating rink, my high school, and my old neighborhood, I couldn't help but think this was the last time I would ever see these places again. As Jay-Z spit his rhymes glorifying the life of a gangster, I knew what it would truly cost. Money, power, and respect, gained through this lifestyle, would only lead to hurt, pain, and regret. Bankrupt and heartbroken, I began to pray...

Seven Days in May:
Transformation and Making Amends
James Cain

Regardless of any abstract extenuating factors that may have perpetuated my inclination for violence, it is because of **me** and **my** lack of self-control, my selfishness, and my choice to shoot an innocent person that our world is short a beautiful human being. My name is James Joseph Cain, I am serving **Life With-Out** the possibility of **P**arole (LWOP) for the senseless and cowardly murder of my ex-girlfriend Judith Pearson on May 19, 2005. It is because of **my** actions that her family and the San Diego community no longer have a parent, a sibling, and a dear friend to share their lives with.

The life experiences that have ultimately led to my criminal behaviors are the result of the path I chose and the decisions I willingly made. I cannot speak for all prisoners as we are as varied as granules of sand in the sea; however, it is clear that at the time I committed my crimes, I was a man immersed in intense inner turmoil. As an adopted child, I was a happy young man and have always felt grateful for my life and amazing family. As the calendar years advanced, my happiness began to deteriorate as my parents uprooted and moved our family six times between 1972 and 1982. These repetitive moves were socially disruptive and destroyed many of the friendships I had made during my formative childhood and adolescent years. Upon moving to each new area, I'd meet new people, make some good friends, form bonds, and then less than a couple years later we'd move and I'd have to repeat this cultural socialization process over again. Perhaps you can imagine how traumatic constantly moving is for a child. Bennet and Castiglioni explain how trauma can result from this type of displacement. "The stronger your identification with a particular space or cultural situation, the more difficult it might be to change spaces without experiencing a lot of discomfort—actual psychological and physiological changes" (Bennet & Castiglioni, 2004). With that, I am now gaining the necessary clarity for understanding the negative effects associated with these moves.

The stress of continuously moving, making new friends and leaving those I cared about behind, surfaced through disruptive behaviors in school as well as a fractured *self*-esteem. The anxiety associated with trying to fit in these new environments left me confused about my personal layers of identity, causing me to lose sight of the *self*. This ultimately led to becoming socially inept, hanging around peers with equally disaffected qualities and experimenting with drugs and alcohol. As this distorted perception of identity began to propagate, I began avoiding my feelings with marijuana and alcohol, which only became worse over time. Although the euphoric escape from the stress of reality allowed me to avoid my problems temporarily, it arrested the development of my communication skills and inhibited my ability to cope with the everyday issues of life. As a result of this sociological deficiency, I developed abusive behaviors, my relationships began to fail and I began to feel less confident about how I perceived my-*self*.

At the time that I had committed this murder, my life was quite literally falling apart. On the surface my life seemed fine, as I was married with two incredible sons, made somewhat of a prosperous living as a plumbing contractor, had a nice home in east county San Diego, and as my own boss, was able to surf at will. Yet, my continued addiction to drugs and alcohol and my poor communication and coping skills continued to thwart my ability to become the man I wanted to be, and needed to be, for my family and myself.

After trying to reconcile through marriage counseling and just two years before we called it quits, I met Judith Pearson on a plumbing service call. Judith was a lovely, Swedish, recently retired account executive for Morgan Stanley. Shortly after meeting, we fell in love, and after an almost two-year love affair she understandably demanded that I leave my broken marriage and get my own place so that we could finally be legit. This was a difficult prospect, for even though my daughter's child support payment from a prior marriage had been modified to zero by the court because her mom had abducted her ten years earlier, the Child Support Division (C.S.D.) had been garnishing 50% of my wages for the past couple of years, regardless of my visitation rights being violated. This placed a tremendous strain on my family and myself, as well as made the consideration of adding the additional expenses of an apartment seemingly impossible. When I inquired with the C.S.D. about my court ordered visitation rights being violated for the past ten years by the mother, their representative told me that my visitation rights weren't their concern. Consequently, shortly before making the final and painful move from the home I shared with my four and six year old sons and wife (**very emotional!**), the D.M.V. informed me that my driver's license was being canceled. A couple days later, my car insurance was canceled and my lienholder was threatening to recall my plumbing truck loan, all as a result of the arrearages accrued during the ten years that my daughter had been abducted (to Canada) by her mother.

In order to catch up on all of these mounting bills as well as pay for a divorce attorney, and earn enough money to move into an apartment, I had to choose to become homeless for a little over two months. This was a very stressful and depressing period in my life. I began seeing a psychologist through my healthcare provider, who in turn referred me to their psychiatrist. The psychiatrist prescribed Prozac to help lessen the stress of my circumstances. While living in my truck for these two months and going through the divorce and child visitation proceedings, I also began attending a Dr. Burns *"Ten Days to Self Esteem"* class while remaining sober. During the course of these classes, and shortly after starting on Prozac, I began having mood swings and other negative side effects attributed to the Prozac, so my doctor modified the previously prescribed amount to see if the negative side effects would change. They didn't.

That month, I had been putting in 16-hour days installing the plumbing for a custom home remodel in La Jolla, a custom plumbing remodel in Golden Hills, and a six unit apartment complex remodel near Balboa Park. I was quite literally burning the candle at both ends. To keep up with the intense work load, I talked myself into believing that it would be ok to temporarily use methamphetamine to keep up with my contracting obligations, at least until I could meet the pending inspections. Finally, I earned enough money to pay all my mounting bills (including my child support payments), get an apartment and meet all my plumbing project deadlines.

That week, shortly after my girlfriend and I celebrated our two-year anniversary, she broke up with me. This was perplexing and heartbreaking because she had just given me an anniversary card telling me, "Just think what we'll have in two more years of days," and there were never any incidents of violence between us, only normal relational challenges. Furthermore, my sole reason for finally giving up on my marriage, making the extremely difficult and emotional move away from my sons and home, and going through all of this financial turmoil and homelessness, was so that my girlfriend and I could finally be together as we had planned.

After weeks of trying to find answers and closure after the ending of our two-year relationship, I decided to continue to self-medicate with meth, Prozac and alcohol. As a result, my behaviors became excessively erratic and totally counterintuitive to the true love I felt for her. This same week one of my closest friends, Tim Jessup, was killed in a Cessna plane crash, my public storage was robbed of approximately $5,000.00 worth of tools and personal items, and once again I had been relying upon drugs and alcohol to deal with my mounting troubles and feelings, the only coping mechanism I knew.

By the 19th of May, I had been up for six nights with only a few hours sleep. And despite hallucinating visually and audibly, I had decided to drive to the La Jolla construction site, at the last moment detouring up Interstate 15 to my ex-girlfriend's home in an attempt to talk with her one last time. After another failed attempt, unintentionally breaking a pane of glass, and her response, "You are going to jail," I returned to my neighborhood, stole two guns from a relative's home and returned to my ex-girlfriends with the irrational intention of attempting to seek closure while armed just in case there was someone there to prevent my attempt. When I entered the garage, seeing her in the running car, I tapped on the driver's window while concealing the gun in my backpack. When she refused to acknowledge me and instead began backing up, I felt broken and at my wits end, senselessly firing one shot into the driver's side window murdering her as her car rolled into the neighbor's driveway across the street. I could hardly believe what I had just done as I had never even held a handgun until that terrible day, and now I had just murdered an innocent human being.

The impact of my actions has been exponential. I have destroyed innumerable people's lives. And though it's irrelevant to the tremendous harm I have caused, I turned myself in, admitted to the crime, and led the arresting officers to where, in a fit of shock, I threw the guns. Moreover, I refused to pursue a trial as I did not want to cause her family, friends, or my own, any further trauma. Neither did I want San Diego tax-payers to have to pay for an expensive capital murder trial when I knew that I was guilty of the crime.

I was so traumatized by shooting and killing this incredible person that I finally stopped a 28 year drug and alcohol addiction that day, and have now been sober for 12 years, 7 months, and 14 days. And even though I knew that Life With-Out would mean I was never going to get out of prison, I have dedicated my life to changing from the man I had become and to trying to understand causation, or how I could have gotten to that point. Since I have been incarcerated, I have participated in multiple self-help classes to confront and correct defects in my character, earned an associate's degree with a business major, and am currently a third of the way into a Communication Studies degree with California State Los Angeles. In *Pedagogy of the Oppressed (2005)*, Paulo Freire writes of the importance for rising above our circumstances in our pursuit of transformation;

"In the incessant struggle to regain their humanity... the oppressed must be able to wage the struggle for liberation, they must perceive the reality of oppression not as a closed world from which there is no exit, but as a limiting situation which they can transform"

I relate Freire's words to my personal quest for transformation within an environment that, according to my sentence, I may never leave unless through God's Grace.

Finally, as a way of making amends, I am using my knowledge learned in C.S.U.L.A. and my desire for change to create proposals for the California Board of Education that will help change the status quo of educational requirements from elementary school through high school. The proposals push for inclusion of Interpersonal/ Intercultural Communication and Personal Finance curriculums to help teach our young people emotional and social intelligence as the means to mitigate bullying and teen suicide and to help deter them from committing future violence, while also teaching them financial intelligence to prepare them for the vital financial decisions that lie ahead. If I had learned these skills through a highly influential, mandatory scholastic curriculum, I believe that I would not have considered violence as an option and ultimately would have been successful in all of my friendships, relationships as well as learned in the financial skills necessary for planning for my future and achieving financial independence. In closing, I leave you with the insightful words of Pincy:

"Character is determined by how we repair the damage."

Compton Black
Donte Williams

PHOTOS AND FRAGMENTS

Healing

Anthony McDuffie

I was told healing is a process, I needed help, but the only help I knew would heal me was God, so I sought God's help like a prospect. Reading biblical words gave me the knowledge and insights to understand my sinful nature, I have purpose now, and I centered my focus inwardly, working on myself like a project. In retrospect, looking back at my old lifestyle, I feel the shame, I feel remorse for people I harmed, unaware of their names. I don't place any blame, but rather hold myself accountable and responsible for my actions, and seek forgiveness for people I caused pain. Poetically, I vent to repent for many of my misdeeds through prayer, and filling my once empty vessel up with knowledge, becoming like the phoenix that rose from the ashes of death, to a rebirth. A seed formed inside of me and I watered that seed with love that took root in the core of my heart, it restored me. The trauma was removed from my psyche, peace replaced criminality. Now that I have went through the process of healing, I will pray for guidance to help heal other people through my testimony, to me that's restorative justice.

Seasons Change (November 6, 2015)
Miguel Velasquez

Spring has come, the sight of green and such beautiful flowers, not to mention the weather awaiting your return, be it whenever

Summer's here, maybe a swim in the ocean, swimming in my emotions…hearts still open

Fall has arrived, leaves from the trees flowing in the sky regretting this fall of mine, becoming friends with time

Winter's here, it gets cold while the ground is frozen, hope my heart doesn't become cold because of the one I've chosen, only your arrival will make up for the seasons stolen.

I wrote this with intentions of expressing myself in a less typical manner. I can see why this can seem like I'm talking to a woman, but in all honesty, I'm not. I'm talking to myself. The person I was before I inherited all these negative features. We were all innocent at one point in our lives. But we allowed things to form our behavior and lifestyle. I know I can't get everything back, but I can get most of it back. Before I can change, I need that same innocence that I had as a kid that allowed myself to be changed negatively. I remember being funny, outgoing, unafraid to ask questions or smile, but that changed at one point. I hope I get back to that.

yourself how can I...
...that. ...So I dont become...
...way. What would I think?

I understand now the severity of...
...and how it brought trauma to you, your...
...the community. The impact my actions have...
...be damaged that I've caused. I wasn't aware...
...that I've learned about myself...
...to hurt anyone else again...
...ize to your family for my...

and October 15, 2005
n LAPD SWAT officer
as I sat atop of
you into the sight of

scared in my life. I've
and have been very
exchanged round
T. And it seems
...d when I

...think about the best
...ant come up with the
...when I become ashamed
...t way to tell you beco-
...y is'nt good enough
...that I will not invest
...lance

James Reyna #V91331

Dear Mrs. Lilly Apardian & family;
First I would like to extend my regards
And am hoping that you are in gre...
...and physically.
...nging this situation to your attention
...ccepting responsibility for and apolog...
...go I made a horrible decision of...
Mr. Mike Apardian life. I n...
...hy for my choices in l...
...ave done. And...
...nd the ripple ef...
Pardian and his lo...

Mr. Mike Apardian Next of Kin L...

Thibodeaux, D
G28407

To the famil
because no o

In October
and alcohol
of the wo
before them
character
before Octo
embarrass
for not

I wa
my beh
Tude o
detrime
at la

my life has always been on the
On March 16, 2012 My life
...fathom the thoughts your family,
...t on that eerie and painful
...ered that establishment armed
...ly ashamed for my role. I
...decision I made that day.
...my actions caused such
...arm that it may have
...rusk, trauma, fear,
...only imagine the
...ll may bare.
...day even

Carrille family
...one of the most difficult letter that I have had to
...tremely embarrassed and ashamed for the hurt
...through when I shot and murdered your son
...and suffering that I have
...I know your son Luis
...I can't exp
...that

I deprived you of you...
your children of a father;
Pardians' grandchildren of a father;
...ved Mr. Apardians' father of a Gran
Mr. Apardians' brothers' and sisters' o
...stand that under no circumstances should
...ve their life taken. I understand the
...to your family and to your friends
...d bring Mr. Apardian back
...and disgusted, for...I
...sing my cha...

...by
...n out
...your
...may
...never

...o your family

Ozzie

...O OUT TO WASTE THIS LETTER TO
...THE PAIN THAT WAS CAUSED DUE TO YOUR
...SORRY YOU DIED BY THE HANDS OF BANGER'S
...AD OF A NATRAUAL DEATH DUE TO NATRAUAL CAUSE...
...Y DESERVES TO DIE THE WAY YOU DIED. NOT ONLY
...T I COULD ONLY IMAGINE HOW TRAMATIZED YOUR K
...TTER WATCHING THEIR FATHER BEEN BEAT UP.

...RAY FOR AND I APOLOGIZE FOR EVERYTHING
...BER 5TH, 2007...

...have empathy with
...they lost and this c
...understands of ha...
...lities for the ta...

...responsibilities so...
...with
...the
...tor
...thou
...my lo

get straight to the point. I do not like you. Words
even begin to describe how I feel. That day when
gunpoint by an masked individual carrying a
has played over and over in my mind like a
peat. Before I met you life seemed so kind.
ll remember those horrifying feelings along
ness and panic being forced to comply with
barked. The line of comands were sheer
membering seeing my life flash in seconds and
nowing if I would ever get the chance to see
was in the pit of my soul. I remember
t prayer to my Higher Power and wishing that
my last day on Earth, but just a simple
veral rounds and saw glass shattering. The
d target - You! I didn't mean to take
ft me no other choice and I
day of my life.
slightest thump. It could be a
to a car backfiring due to
g counseling
to get t

about what
was the wor
e sharp pain enter
my breathing as the
g me to the ground. I was
the terror of not knowing if Y

in the back of that truck taking me to
blood that I was drifting in & out of con
rified. My breath was fading & I was terribly
ted to save my life. Did you know my life & futu
s that night? I thought of my family, realizing I
roken they will be to find out what happened to
s & did not deserve this. All I wanted to do was su
l left me, fearfully & helplessly realizing that I wo
nizing death. I didn't deserve to die Brian. It was t
nce at a full life, get married, have a child, who's going to
hen they can't help themselves? Are you? All I wanted was
you & your friends but you viciously took away my life & futu
at, whatever your doing, everytime you think of your own fami
of what you did to me & how you get the chance to live your life
any remorse for what you've done, I ask that you turn t

s do forgive, so that
and anger.

hate and anger. I can't st
me and my family tremen
anger within.

Arturo. I have forgiven.
is forever printed in my mind. Just as it
mind of my father, mother, aunt, and love ones.
graph of the last days of my life.
My parents struggled emotionally, physically, an
ly, because they could not do anything to help me. They
me eachother for what happen.
I fought hand because I wanted to
ly to take car

ds of my seven survivors, survivors
o be known as a victim.

I allowed anger, anxiety, depression
my judgement and I made some
ons of my entire life. I knew
had some serious defects of
uld have been dealt with long
and for that I am ashamed and
ccept full unlimited responsibility
Those issues sooner.

ly careless, wreckless and selfish in
ow understand the impact and magni
e and how I contributed to the
community and the entire country

c to the feelings of all effected by
the victims, to the community
ders and my own

The Past Is Not the Past: Hyperincarcerated Poor People of All Colors Cry Out to Us

Jeff Stein

"We ate the berries they said were poisonous, heard the songs they said would drive us mad, watched the movies and read the books they said would corrupt us; we fought in battles they did in no way sanction—though they were relevant to us; only their wars are right, good, and just.

And we followed prophets they did not endorse or enshrine; they said we were led astray; we were never enfranchised, and so we made our own way. One by one and by the millions we ran afoul of what is good and right; men, women, and children (yes, children☹) covered in everlasting darkness and chains that bind.

But we are not alone. Those who have gone before us surely know; Whether already in one of your **relocation centers** or waiting to go—we languish apart from and among you—alive and yet unborn"

(Inspired by Professor Elizabeth Houston and Common)

Sacred Places

Dimitri Gales

Welcome to this golden place,
Where our energy and love is delivered on golden plates.
Our aspirations are driven by hope and faith,
This is... our sacred place.

This is a place we've conquered,
This is our place of trust,
This is our place of comfort,
This is a place for us.

We come here free of wearing masks,
And healing those hearts which were once black.
This is our community,
Built on love, trust, respect and unity.

Reaching For The Light
Kenneth Webb

RECONNECTED
Part Two

Cheeps

Duncan Martinez

This is not about me, I am not important here. Do not get lost in who I am or why I am writing. It is about them, and what they were able to do. How they changed lives, how they allowed for change. I don't matter, never forget that.

We first met her in a paper bag. I remember the first look, the way she stared deeply into my eyes, a pleading look—absolute need. I also remember the way he took to her so quickly, the way she invaded his heart... she was, frankly, irresistible.

Eyes a deep hazel, but dark, almost black. In the right light they looked green, or hinted of it in an odd sense—as if there had been green there just a few moments before, but it had washed away... like a smell that is barely there: gone, but unforgettable. She had beautiful eyes.

Of course, we never knew for certain if she was a she at all. There wasn't time to find out, and as the years have gone by I have gone back and forth, but right now I like to think that she was a she.

No matter what, she was beautiful.

She was ours.

Aaron had never had anything like her before, never been in that sort of situation—certainly not as an adult. It was an odd paradigm, where we all fit into the mix, but none of that mattered: everything we did was about one simple thing— love. We loved her as intensely as anyone can love anything. She was a part of us in a way that only family can be.

Cheeps was awesome.

The paper bag opened to four of them, little balls of down and fluff. Eyes searching for something they could understand. Each went a separate way, and each to a different end. All of them sad, in every sense. She was three days old, and her nest had been removed from an air-conditioning unit or some such. The tech that had done the job simply threw it away. Four baby birds tossed into a trashcan for no reason other than their parents had thought the nest brilliantly placed. I hate to think of what her parents went through... the anguish of their nest being found and taken, and there being nothing they could do about it.   Nothing.

But, the chicks were saved and put into that paper bag, four siblings tucked into a towel in an alien place. Four birds that were lucky to still be alive.

When I looked in, Cheeps looked right at me. There was no question which of the four I wanted, no question that I had been selected, or that we had been. She came home to a place where we had no idea how such a small thing could be so gigantic; how much of our lives she would take over; how deeply she would be set into our hearts.

We knew nothing of caring for a baby sparrow. She was so small; she took a nap in those early days in my ear, her entire body fitting neatly into the depression. She was so cute, so amazingly cute, that she created a soft spot within us, forging a bond that we were helpless to defend against. And, if I had any chance of fighting it after that initial look, I was hopelessly lost once she went belly down for a nap in the hollow of my sternum. It was amazing. Birds grouse their feathers as they get ready to nap, lowering themselves slowly, sometimes on one leg; they nestle down and even tuck their heads under a wing. Sometimes it takes minutes to work into that position, while other times it can be fast—the rhyme and reason of it escapes me. But, when they do it really fast it is cool to watch. Having a tiny little bird with head tucked and her feathers fluffed out in a giant ball, fall asleep **on you**... it's beautiful. And, if you ask Aaron, I'm sure he can recall the moment where she took him, too. I'm sure it is as burned into him as that was for me.

We had to make a syringe to feed her, and concoct the right mix of foods. The barrel of a pen filled with wet bread and peanut butter worked perfectly. Feedings every hour or two for weeks. Imagine the work of those parents when they had four! Imagine the volume of insects or whatever they would have to go through, not to mention the extra food they would need to eat to feed themselves. It's astounding to think about. They are so small, sparrows, especially the babies, but they are truly amazing creatures.

The first one died the first night. Maybe it was stress, maybe the guy did something wrong, who can say. In so many ways, we were making it up as we went along—we were not ornithologists, not even close. But, the next morning she was dead asleep, literally. As most sparrows don't make it six months, at least we had managed to give the poor chick a little love before it died.

We ordered a book about small birds that helped with a ton of things. It ranged from basic training to actual minor surgeries. Fortunately, Cheeps never needed that!

Cheeps grew quickly, and by the time her down started to fall out, she had almost doubled in size. She couldn't fly at all, but was adventurous wherever we let her roam. We carefully checked her for mites and a whole slew of problems outlined in our book—she was disease-free and very healthy. I kept her in a small, open box on my bed, right next to my head. It was the very bottom of a twelve pack of sodas, with a washcloth as bedding and it was twenty times too big. She would perch on the edge, whichever edge was closest to me. Then, one night, she hopped off the edge and onto my head. Burrowing down into my hair as if in a nest, she went to sleep right beside my ear. She slept on my head every night for the rest of her life.

Imagine a golf ball of warmth tucked into your hair. You have to be aware of it when you move, roll over, what have you. You become attached in a new way, a part of this wondrous thing. Every time I would move at night, I would shift gently—just a tad—so she would know I was about to move, and then as I rolled over she would walk with me until she had her new spot. It was awesome. Every morning when I awoke to that... every morning it was awesome.

The second one was killed by an errant foot. The little one was allowed to roam free in their house, to be a part of the family. A poorly placed foot and that was that. I don't think it was even a month old, but, like it's brother before it, at least it got a period of love.

As she grew into her first set of feathers, there was a problem. The feathers on her left wing came in badly. We were never sure what caused it, but that set of feathers was basically useless. She could not fly, couldn't even really glide. Cheeps could hop to the floor from my bed, but could not get back up. The positive out of this was that it meant we were privileged enough to get to help her do everything. We did not complain.

I was eating popcorn one day and she was on her perch by the window. She started cheeping, of course, but then bobbing up and down excitedly. I put my arm out and she hopped along my arm almost too fast to see. As she ate the popcorn from my tongue I could not help but smile. Her glee was so impressive that we ate what we knew she would like.

We built her a cage for when we were not at home, and it opened in a way that the top became a shelf beside a window for her. That became her spot, when she wanted time to herself. Depending on what we were doing, she could see us from there—it was a great vantage point. She could look outside, but mostly watch over us. Her eyes would slowly work into a nap as she relaxed, but pop open to check—she was not going to miss anything. We would stock the cage with clover and popcorn, two of her favorite things. She didn't mind the cage, but you could tell the best thing was when she was with us. She was a flock bird and we were her flock.

Again, awesome. We use that word so frequently, throw it around like a trivial thing: I do not mean that, I mean that she filled us with awe in a sense that we had never really experienced. She was our child, friend, family. We were closer as friends because of the fortune to have her in our lives. To eat popcorn with a bundle of joy sitting on your shoulder cheeping for a nibble... the excitement, the joy, the companionship. I will always have a special place in my heart (and on my head) for Cheeps.

Our world became hers, our every decision made with her in mind. She was smaller than a golf ball, as I said, but a part of everything we did and were. I don't know how else to explain the depth of our bond, how much of life was about Cheeps, but I imagine it was like raising a newborn. Everything was different, but it was also better, fuller.

Cheeps died on a Sunday, in the morning, in a terrible way. We went to chow, so we put her into the cage. Sunday breakfast is one of the best in prison. We left her in the cage with a string of popcorn and a bundle of clover. We'd be back in less than half an hour, but would never see her again. This tiny thing that had invaded our lives, taken so much but given so much more, depended on us, and there was nothing we could do to save her. We didn't even know she needed saving.

We came home and as Aaron closed the door, I noticed the cage was empty. We cannot just open our doors, that's not how it works. We searched the cell, thinking maybe she had gotten out... but the cage was still tight, the lid closed. Someone had done this and we knew it. We began to yell at the door for the tower officer to open it up. He would not. Our child was gone, and we began a period of explosive emotions—raging and freaking out, losing it, and yet clinging to irrational hopes that sprang forward as we raged behind the closed door—trapped in a cell, a reality, by a loss. Here is what we saw:

An officer that does not work in our building was up in the tower with the regular. He smiled a grim smile as he peeked our way. Our regular was clearly very uncomfortable. After a bit, the visitor left, taking a plastic bag with him. The bag was ballooned out, yet mostly empty, and we could not make out what was inside. It was Cheeps.

The visitor told the floor officer that he took her outside and let her go. He told her that she flew away, gesturing up into the air. We know for a fact that was a lie. When we finally got out, knowing she couldn't fly, we went outside and called for her. She knew her name, responded to it, and would hop right to us when called. We searched for hours, until we found out the truth.

A friend was out at yard when the visitor left. He watched him walk straight to the toilet on the yard and flush a plastic bag down. He thought it odd that something like that would happen. He said the bag was ballooned up, and that the visitor looked giddy as he did it. Whether he was giddy at the idea of our pain or at the act of murder, we never knew.

Aaron lost it and wanted blood. I used our friendship as a way of dealing with my emotions: Aaron had a chance to go home, and I did not. Aaron had a chance to be a human being again, and doing anything in a situation like this would jeopardize that. I talked him off the ledge, so to speak, used him as a focus to help me through the anguish. Cheeps had been murdered... an irony that was not lost on us, considering that that was the crime we were both in prison for. She was just a bird, a tiny little thing that you've seen a million of in your life. A tiny little thing that was ours, and we hers... a tiny little thing that was doing no harm to anyone at all.

Perspective. There is no bringing her back, but what is there? How do you make that right? How do you reconcile that in any sort of sense? Reality is that when we took her in she was destined to die. That day or some other, and we did the best we could to do the best we could. We could not save her forever, nor could we bring her back. It hurt in a way that only loss can, that unfillable emptiness. But, I would not trade that time, no way: we were lucky enough to have had her at all—to have communed with her, to have been her flock.

I'd like to say we got over it quickly, but it has been over five years and I still get choked up just thinking of her. She never got old enough to have her full adult coat—so we never knew for sure if she was a he or a she. She would have died in that trashcan and we were able to give her months of intense love, months of family. She gave us a lifetime of caring, left an imprint that will never go way. It cannot. A part of us died that Sunday morning, just as a part of us learned about love in the weeks before. We are more for both love and loss, forever more.

Aaron went home, went back to the real world and matter again. He is doing really well and loving the opportunity. The world could have so easily missed out on his contributions, because he loved a bird. We loved a bird. That love is what a sociopath tried to use as torture by flushing Cheeps down a toilet. Last we heard, he had retired and was miserable. Karma, I guess.

The final bird was released because the men that had him were worried that the same thing might happen to them. Buddy was a boy, and stayed with us a little longer. After they let him go, they would see him most days. That lasted a month or so, and then nothing. Like so many sparrows in the wild, Buddy didn't last very long.

To this day, when I am asleep and I go to roll over, I make one motion first so that Cheeps can know what is coming. Some nights I can almost feel her move with me. I don't know which is worse, the absence or that ghostly feeling that reminds she is gone.

I Promise

Allen Dean Burnett II

Dear Little Dean,

God loves you and so do I. *I promise I do.* I am writing to you because I want to tell you a few things that are going to help us along the way. In a few days mom is going to wake you up early in the morning and get you ready for school. She's going to be upset, but its okay, Little Dean, she's not mad at you. You see, yesterday our kindergarten teacher sent a note home pinned to your shirt. The note asked mom to come in for a meeting; the teacher thinks something is wrong with us because you won't read or talk in class.

It's okay though, Little Dean, we're fine. I know what's wrong—I'm going to explain for you. I'll tell them that dad died, and you don't understand what that means. I'll explain to them that you found him overdosed and you're still scared. I'll explain for you. *I promise.* I will explain it all.

I need you to do me a favor and try not to be sad—okay. I was sad for us so *you* don't have to be. I need you to be strong and when mom sits you down and starts yelling because she can't find the pick for your hair—it's not your fault; she is hurt and frustrated. She misses dad just as much as you do, so when she starts crying you tell her, "I will take care of you momma." Okay? Just like that. Got it? That will help her stop crying, and when she takes you to school, you *be brave* because mom is going to ask you to read. She is going to put a book in front of you and tell you, "Read the first page, show her you can read." And when you do, teacher will be so surprised by how well you read, at how strong you are, she will leave us alone. I promise they will.

Little Dean we are going to have a lot of hard times, people are going to let us down, hurt us and lie to us; kids are going to call us names like *stupid, ugly,* and *dummy,* but don't be sad because *it aint even true.* I was already sad for you so you don't have to ever be. I'm going to make all the bad choices for us too, and I'm going to be held accountable for those choices, but you little Dean, *you are going to be fine*—you know why? Because you are *so smart,* you are *handsome,* and you are *loved.* I'm going to take care of you; I'm going to guide you through. I promise.

Now you have to do something for me; don't stop reading, don't stop trying, and don't stop learning. Be nice to yourself and don't ever be afraid to ask for help when you don't understand something. God loves you and so do I. *I promise I do.* I will write again soon.

Love, *Yourself*

Dear Little Dean,

Do you remember me? It's been a while since I've written to you. I think about you daily, I promise I do. I see you took my advice and you are still reading and learning. That's good. *Don't ever stop.* It's going to help us, I promise it will.

I want to share a little more with you. What I'm about to write may be a little scary, but you need to know *everything* so I can explain it all later; now pay attention—okay? One night when you are about 10 years old, you are going to wake up to the sound of mom screaming your name. Her screaming is going to send chills down your spine and make it hard for you to breathe, and when you see her and Step-dad in the hallway fighting you are going to become confused and scared. Now you are going to want to help, but you don't know how. So, I'm going to tell you what to do. Mom is going to try to get away from him, but he won't let her go. He is going to press his forearm on her neck and point a gun at her face. Mom is scared and crying. She is going to beg him to let her go, but he's not going to do it. Mom is going to tell you to *"Call 911!" But Don't move, not a muscle.* You see, Step-dad is drunk again, and he is going to point the gun at you, too. He's going to yell at you and tell you to *"Go lay down!"* but remember your promise to mom, *"I will take care of you momma."* So you stand there and--*You watch him*--and you don't move or say a word. And I promise he will let her go. He will leave her alone. I promise he will.

What's happening with mom and Step-dad is not your fault. You see, they are struggling. They are struggling to communicate, to understand each other, and they are struggling to love one other. They are hurt on the inside, and they are hurting each other. And sometimes when people are hurting, they hurt other people; even the people they love. So, I don't want you to be sad because this is not your fault, and please don't be angry. I was angry enough for both of us.

Little Dean, I need you to understand something else; Step-dad drinks all the time, and he is using drugs, too. He is unhappy. Some days he is sad and mean, and other days he's nice. And when he's nice he's going to take you places and buy you books and you are going to love him so much. But when he is mean, he is going to punch you. He believes that he is making you tough, he doesn't realize how much he is hurting us. He is going to call you *dumb* because it takes you a little longer to figure things out, and that is going to make you want to stop trying but *Don't ever give up*. It is going to be hard, and sometimes it is going to hurt, but don't ever give up. I'm going to help you through it all, I promise, and eventually everything will be okay. I will write you soon. God loves you and so do I. I promise I do.

Love, *Yourself*

Dear Little Dean,

Today someone asked me who I thought was the most influential person in my life growing up. I immediately thought of Step-dad, and I remembered it was time to write you again. One day soon Little Dean, you are going to be writing to me and helping others by sharing our story. I promise. Watch—you'll see.

One day an older boy is going to call you names and shove you to the ground in front of all your friends. You are going to try to force yourself to forget this day ever happened. It is an awful memory, but it is a very important one. It is a memory that is going to help put everything in perspective for you. I promise it will.

Now let me help you. That day you are going to be embarrassed and try to run inside of the house crying, but Step-dad is going to be standing in the front door, watching everything. He is not going to let you inside. Instead, he is going to hand you a marble ashtray and order you to go and hit the boy in the face. He is going to yell at you and tell you, *"Stop crying, or I'm gonna give you something to cry about!"* You are going to be scared and ashamed but you really want Step-dad to love you. You're more afraid of Step-dad than you are of what he wants you to do to the boy. But you are going to be brave; you are always brave Little Dean. You are going to walk up to this boy and tell him, *"Don't ever touch me again."* But just telling him not to touch you ever again is not good enough for Step-dad, and he is going to let you know. As soon as you walk into the house, he is going to kick you and whip you with his belt. He is going to snatch you up by your arms and pull you to his face and you will smell alcohol on his breath and what he says will stay with you forever. *"When I tell you to do something, you do it! If anybody messes with you, you pick something up and knock the shit out of them. And if you don't, I'm gonna whup your ass again."* It's not your fault Little Dean, Step-dad really thinks he is helping. He is wrong.

Three years later, when you are 14 years old, you are going to hurt someone very badly. A boy is going to say something to you in class that you don't like. You are going to feel embarrassed and challenged, and you are going to hit him in the head with a stapler. When the principal asks you why you did it, you are going to tell him exactly what you learned from Step-dad, *"He was messing with me."* You are going to be kicked out of school and placed on juvenile probation for assault and battery.

The next year you are going to be arrested for possession of a handgun. Step-dad is going to turn you in, and when he asks you why you have a gun, you are going to remind him of what he taught us, *"In case someone messes with me."* Eventually, you are going to start drinking—just like Step-dad. You are going to become angry, and depressed, just like Step-dad. You are going to stop caring about yourself or anyone else. You are going to hurt people. By the time you are 18 years old, you will be arrested and sent to prison for the rest of our life. For murder.

I know these things are tough for you to read, but it's the truth. It's not going to be easy, Little Dean. The shame, the regret, and the remorse, are going to corner you in and eat at you. It is going to make it hard for you to live with yourself, but, Little Dean, you are going to be okay. Remember I promised that I would take care of you. Remember? I told you that I would be held accountable for all our choices. I am going to take responsibility for everything, and I am going to guide you through it all. You are never going to be alone. I promise.

Now, Little Dean, you are going to have to do something for us. You are going to have to forgive yourself and forgive Step-dad; this will help you change our story. I know you can do it because you are smart and brave. Once you do, you will begin to honor the people that you've hurt, you will become an honorable man, a leader of honorable men, and never *ever* harm anyone again. Got it? You need to help me share our story to help people understand, and then maybe, little boys won't have to grow up like us. They can change their stories too. We will show them that change is possible. Okay?

Things are going to work out for you Little Dean, I promise. You are going to be fine. You are going to be a great husband and father and mom and step-dad are going to be so proud of you, I promise they will. Just never give up and never stop trying. Oh, and one more thing, write me and tell me everything you have done and everything you are going to do, and I promise we are going to be just fine. Watch. God loves you Little Dean and so do I. I promise I do.

Love, *Yourself*

For Steven Eric Brannon, Step-dad

Positive Transition

Terry Bell

For a long time I didn't know my sentence

Thought I had 25 to life, couldn't distinguish the difference

Between life without and life with parole

"You will never see the streets again" is what I was told

Sent off to prison feeling like I lost everything

And my support group soon felt like a one-man team

Friends faded, some family, my girl left me for another

The pain deepened within this broken-hearted brother

Seemed like all at once my causative factors hit me

I recognized the feelings but didn't understand the history

Abandonment, lack of love, verbal abuse

Internal triggers of feeling devalued, all derived from my youth

Housed on a 180 where growth was far from everyone's mind

Rehabilitation's foreign and plenty had accepted their time

Where agony took victory and mindsets were affected

And the behavior of this population reflected

Apathy dominated, and yes my heart hardened

My humanity became lost and my perception darkened

Paranoia consumed my brain and trust became obsolete

Emotionally numb, couldn't cry, left my growth incomplete

This sad way of living carried on for years

The cycle became broken shortly after housed here

On this P.P.F. yard, where my darkness transformed to light

Here, I discovered the true meaning of having insight

I learned how to incorporate tools to keep my emotions in check

Along with the origin of my character defects

I discovered change is possible and it's okay to be a little nervous

Rehabilitation starts within and spills out onto the surface

Learned how to reject the false label, dig deep and find the truth

Gratefully educated through *Men For Honors'*, Helping Youth

I developed a new mindset and restored my humanity

By the grace of God been blessed with physical health and my sanity

They say a man isn't supposed to cry; that's a lie

Since changed, I've let an abundance of tears run down my eyes

It feels good to feel whole and know I have a soul

And put to rest learned behavior, regardless what I was told

I went from studying moves on the yard for my survival

To studying work from school for my finals

Was told education is key, so constantly I build my mental

And refuse to let incarceration conceal my potential

Remaining mindful of my future to keep my present on track

To be reminded how far I came, is the only time I look back.

To Imagine Angels

John Purugganan

I have lived behind bars for almost 30 years now. My fourth year in brought times where I didn't know if I'd see a fifth; moments when it was difficult to care, one way or the other. One of those times was on a cold Autumn morning, here in this desert valley.

I sat alone at the north end of the yard. Waiting. I worked on the yard crew. The day before, Duke, the inmate lead man, and I had words. A petty dispute over a waterspout turnkey, of which he was in charge, and which I used every day to complete my assigned tasks. The details of our moronic exchange are not worth repeating. Suffice it to say, agitated stirrings went unchecked as I awaited Duke and the water key the following morning. The fact that he was late had me nursing fresh frustration with mounting anger from the previous day.

Years before, in the county jail, as the cocaine left my system, the savagery of my crime began sinking in. I'd killed a man, and the horrific reality of my atrocious actions went far beyond committing the ultimate criminal act. I caused immeasurable pain and sorrow in the lives of everyone who loved the man whose life I took. Together with that is what my unforgivable crime did to my own loved ones, especially to my children. It crushed them. I broke their hearts.

As is often the case when a man realizes how far he has fallen, I longed to distance myself from that person who wrought such devastation, who caused so much grief. I knew I could never make up for what I did, still I vowed to live the rest of days endeavoring to make amends, to become a better person, to restore my humanity.

Of course, these thoughts were far from me as I waited for Duke that morning. My ego and self-righteous indignation only fueled thoughts of vengeance. I ignored my inner voice, telling me there had to be a better way of handling this. I'd resigned to give this guy what he'd been asking for all week.

No sooner had my inner voice faded to a whispered sigh that I heard another voice – and it wasn't in my head. It came from directly above me, the chirping of a bird. Perched high up on the razor wire that topped the cinderblock wall, was a parakeet; the same type I used to see at the pet shop when I was a child.

With its egg yolk yellow-feathered breast and vibrant aquamarine shaded wings, achingly incongruent with this dreary massive prison construct, it was like being visited by a tiny miracle.

"Hey, you," I said, and it chirped as if in response. I asked if it was here to see me and the bird instantly chirped again, a measured, harmonious recital, as if it was trying to tell me something. I told it I'd been having a bad week and expressed my gratitude for its coming my way.

This earned another lengthy melodic response. You could easily mark it off as the imaginings of a lonely man condemned to life without the possibility of parole, but I'll be damned if the tone of that pretty bird's tweets didn't sound cheerful.

The solid metal gate that fronted the work exchange building grinded open and out stepped Miss Owens, a guard. She saw me sitting on the cement walkway and the parakeet perched on the razor wire above, and cried out, "Look at that!" At the sound of her voice the bird flew off.

It must have been someone's pet that had escaped its cage and strayed untold miles to sing a few notes of encouragement to me, a fellow cage-dweller. Coincidence? Or was it something more? I noticed a distinct change in myself, my spirit felt uplifted, inexplicably cleansed in some odd way.

Duke didn't show up for work that morning. I saw him later, during yard program. Without any looks or prompting on my part, he came up to me and summarily apologized, said he'd been having a bad week. I knew about bad weeks. He offered an out-stretched hand, and I shook it.

***

Five months later. Once again, my spirit had grown weary, and just as suddenly as the first time, another feathered creature found its way to me. I'd been up all night, missing my children, loathing myself for abandoning them. Wallowing in misery, conjured demons of despair taunted me through the sleepless hours.

The last thing I remembered before nodding out and being jarred awake as "Chow Release!" sounded over the P.A. system was the soft blue-gray glow of dawn illuminating the thin vertical rectangle window.

I hadn't slept 10 minutes.

Several hours later. I'd been to breakfast. Made a yard crew appearance. Came back to my cell with the notion that I could still manage to get some writing done.

I'd been sitting at my desk for I don't know how long, staring at the small

LCD screen on my Smith Corona 200 typewriter when a fluttering motion in my peripheral caused me to raise my eyes to the six-inch wide, four-foot high window. Right outside the reinforced glass on the inclined ledge, sat a baby owl. It seemed to be peering right at me but had to be looking at its own image, as the outside of the window was covered with reflection tape.

No taller than the window was wide, the owl couldn't see me but it could obviously hear me: it kept looking around at the sound of my voice, which came from behind its own reflection on the tape. I removed the typewriter, climbed on the desktop, sat cross-legged and gazed at the tiny wonder.

I'd never seen an owl around here, there are no trees in prison, and virtually no trees for miles beyond the fatal electrified fence. So where did it come from? Did it live in a nest? Was there a worried-frantic mama owl out there scouring the neighborhood?

Forty-five minutes later. Dayroom program in progress. Several prisoners stopped by my cell. I presented my visitor. This generated some excitement. Soon I had a crowd gathered around my perforated iron metal door.

Three and a half hours later. My very superstitious Vietnamese cellie returned from school. One look at the fledgling in the window and he cried, "Bad luck! Bad luck." Apparently owls were bad omens in his culture. My suggestion to the contrary was not well-received. He grabbed his shower gear and headed for the shower. It was a long shower, the owl was still perched on the ledge when my cellie came back.

Thank goodness our building was first to be released for dinner, the ordeal would be resolved before my cellie returned again. I stayed behind to prolong my vigil with the owl for as long as I could. By the time the upper tier of cells was released – with all the metal doors banging shut – my day-long companion had flown away.

I had been grateful for its presence, though I wasn't terribly saddened to see him go. He had to get on with his life just as I had to go get on with mine.

This prison compound boasts 20 identical housing units, each containing 100 cells, for a total of 2,000 identical cell windows. All these windows and the baby owl chose mine. Simply another coincidence? Possibly. But same as with the parakeet's visit, I like to think the appearance of the owl was the result of a deliberate intention. Romanticism and mysticism. It lends great solace to believe that *something* sent a baby owl – a nocturnal creature – in the light of day, to assure me I wasn't alone in my darkest hour the night before.

A quarter century later. These cold hard walls are just as high. The razor-laced wire is every bit as sharp. The electric fence is deadly as ever. But when my spirit needs healing I can still recall those feathered messengers, and it gladdens my heart to imagine angels truly do have wings.

I Didn't Know

Jamon Carr

I didn't know

That I could victimize myself, falsely imprison myself…

Behind bars of false and foolish pride, lust, greed and

Anti-social traditions.

I didn't know

I didn't know

That I was binding my youth…

The hindrance of so much potential and promise,

For royal linen that's stained with white paisley print.

Royal, Huh!!!

It was just a color with a mirage of a false prestige.

I didn't know

I didn't know

It was all an illusion,

The honor, the love, the set…

The one for all, all for one,

I was so naive.

I didn't know

I didn't know

That existing and living can feel like polar opposites,

When they're the same…

That's just a side effect of existing in a

Manufactured reality.

          I didn't know

I didn't know

That I would become an advocate for that youth,

I am harnessing that potential and promise

For great uses.

          I didn't know

I didn't know

That I would become a voice for gang prevention,

Exposing their lives to heal our society

And save our youth.

          I didn't know

I didn't know

But now I do, my mission in life is to serve God, Be a service to

Others and father the at-risk youth.

I'll be their father, if there's no one there to love'em.

Fathering the fatherless.

I didn't know, but now I do!

Silence

Spoon Jackson

Blessed in silence
And an unsmiling look
I am often judged

But, it's the seeds
Within the apple
That matter

A magnificent sunset
Makes no sound
Yet it speaks to the world

Stars reflecting
In a midnight sky
Have no voice, yet they are heard

Clouds form in silence
And float softly in the air
Only to speak to refresh the land

I tend to be silent
So that I may listen and see myself
And what is in nature evolving around me

Instilled in every seedling
Reaching for the stars
Is the sweet healing love of the universe.

Dear Kendrick

Jason Keaton

Dear Kendrick,

Hey Bro. I wonder what you're doing right now. You might be on your way overseas to put on a concert for thousands of fans. Maybe you're in the studio laying down another hit. The thought of your success brings great pride and joy to my life. As for me, I am in California State Prison Los Angeles in the education department. I just finished a paper for my English class and here I am now writing to you. Soon, I'll be hitting this yard full of gang members and convicted murderers to go work out. It's crazy to think about how different our lives turned out, the different experiences we have had and the places we have seen, yet here we are, still pushing COMPTON, but now for very different and more positive reasons than we did before.

I wanted to take the opportunity to share my appreciation for all you are and all that you do. You are a true friend who has helped change my life in many ways. Our lives took different turns after high school. You made good decisions and used your talents to bring about change in the world. I made bad ones, bringing about destruction and pain to the community I claimed I loved and countless families. However, I have taken charge of my life and am back on the correct course. Since my incarceration, I have matured and learned to accept responsibility for my past as well as take responsibility for my future. I admit that it has been a hell of a journey with a lot of bumps, but knowing I put myself here has been the drive I needed to change my life and come out a better person. Oh, by the way, I also graduated from college and now am earning my bachelors with Cal State Los Angeles. Would you have ever thought that was possible? Me? A college boy? Miracles do happen. Lol.

You may not know this, but you have been a part of my journal every step of the way. You have been one of the biggest and most positive influences in my life. Watching you succeed has been inspiring. You have motivated me to work hard, stay persistent, and to bring hope to others with my life experiences. You have taught me what it truly means to love COMPTON. You have inspired me to find my purpose in life and I have. COMPTON will not be the reason I fail, but rather the foundation I stand tall on as I reach for my own dreams and success. I've found comfort in you reminding me that, IT'S GONE BE ALRIGHT, and for that and so much more, I thank you.

Your music is high power and has got me through a lot. There are times when I sit in my cold cell and feel like giving up. Then I turn up one of your tracks and it keeps me focused on the bigger picture. It reminds me that I am so much more than my CDC# and these prison blues. I am a child of God, a son of COMPTON, and a man molded by my experiences and in charge of my own destiny. Thank you for your conversations as well. As I read the wisdom of the prophets and Holy Books, I find that your words have been just as encouraging. You are an amazing person, an incredible friend. See you soon. From one SON of COMPTON to another bringing light into the darkness. Much love, gratitude and admiration.

Always,
Jason K.

Dear Kendrick

Compton Children

Jason Keaton

Compton, a place of proud feeling,

A place of sad feeling,

A place filled with both happy children and mad children.

A place where hope is low but crime is high,

Where the struggle is real and families barely get by.

The fathers are missing, kids are wondering "why?"

They can't focus in school from all that's on their minds.

They lack nurture and they lack love.

So they look for it within—

the Crips & Bloods.

Hugs…could prevent thugs!

Love…could prevent blood!

I understand you because I am you!

Same shame, same pain, same story, same dream!

I understand you because I am you.

So I'm coming back to help you before your decisions condemn you

to a life of regret from learning the ripple effect

and having to spend life in prison for something you'll never forget!

I love you, Compton Children.

My Faith Restored

Jack McFadden

I wake up around 4:30. I clean and try to stretch out the old muscles but mostly it is time to catch up on paperwork and plan for the new day with the dogs. I walk out to the sound of dogs barking, barking with happiness to see their trainers coming to get them. I watch my Paws For Life brothers put aside whatever is going in their lives to love their dogs, to take care of them in a way that has touched even this old hardened heart. I smile as I watch men debate over the best way to brush and groom their dog. I watch men try to convince the guy who passes out dog treats how "their dog needs more" treats, or toys, for this or that very serious reason, all because they love their dog. I have watched men walk miles with their dogs, men who would much prefer sitting and eating a honeybun or candy bar in their cell. Yes, because they love their dog!

I watch men take care of these amazing animals for hours and hours, and for no pay. Most of these men, myself included, have LWOP so we are not doing this to get out of prison. We are doing this because we love these dogs so much that we have dedicated ourselves and our time to helping them grow into dogs that will be adopted into families that will love them as much as we do.

Karma Rescue brings dogs to us that are sometimes abused and neglected in ways that I don't even want to mention. These dogs need love and a lot of attention. It is a lot of hard work; many long hours are needed to bring these dogs back to life and to show to them that not everyone in this world will hurt them. I've watched not just one or two, but every single one of these men in this program get down on the floor with these dogs not only to earn their trust, but to show them with their actions that they love them.

I have watched this, round after round, and each time a group of dogs goes out of those gates, a part of me leaves with them. I admit, it is HARD watching them go, but it is their time; it is time for them to be free and go to their new homes, where they will be loved for the rest of their lives. I watch my friends and brothers in the PFL program and I have learned that we have not lost our humanity, it is still there, and we just need a reason to let it out. After decades in prison, I have finally found something to dedicate myself to, something bigger than myself that gives back to the community. I have the opportunity to help train dogs that will someday become Service Dogs for Veterans. Nothing affirms the value of life more than these wonderful dogs, whether Service animals or just friends, and the unconditional love they give us in return.

Those of you who have been in prison for many years understand how easy it is to lose your faith in humanity. The days slowly blur into one long fog that never seems to end, full of stupidity and the boring repetition of prison life. But when Paws For Life came along, my eyes opened up to a whole new world. It now has meaning.

Becoming

Dara Yin

Thirty years ago, in a faraway land, there was a lad named Shawn. He had fantastical dreams and aspirations of living a spectacular life. He wanted wealth and to travel the world. However, there were things that Shawn struggled with, that he did not quite understand. Feeling empty, wanting more than he had, he knew not who he was. Although he had a mother, a brother, and two sisters, all who loved him dearly, his thoughts were so consumed with his selfishness and abandonment by his father that Shawn did not see the love.

In the days of his childhood, Shawn would explore the fields around his village until the night fell heavy. His mother and brother warned him to stay away from the hooligans in the village. Shawn did not heed their warnings. After all, why should he listen to a mother who was a drunkard and a brother who was never around? All he did was punish Shawn when he did something wrong. At least that's how Shawn saw it.

Shawn became a thief early in his age stealing water pistols from the market. He was often ridiculed by other children for having broken toys and torn clothes. This brought shame and anger into Shawn's heart. As Shawn grew older, an adolescent he became. He did not enjoy his schooling as good grades brought him no fame. He thought it better to rob and sell forbidden drugs, this brought recognition, something he craved. There was a void in Shawn that he could not understand. A father, he never had. Everything he wanted, he could never have. Whether it be materialistic or love, he looked and looked, unable to fill this unknown void.

He joined the ruffians that his mother and brother warned him about. Here he felt command, here he felt purpose, and here he felt belonging. Or so he thought. That oasis was not as it seemed, a swamp covered in gold. His mother did not like his decision and cursed him heavy, his mother tells him that she wished him never born. He did not join the ruffians to make her angry but with her words of venom, his heart filled with hate and disdain.

* * *

He hunts for treasures, he fights every fight. He takes to the world all the pain in his life. Another boy killed, another boy jailed, Shawn finds himself in a cold, dark, cell.

The boy, murdered, in cold blood, a spirit with dreams, aspirations, and love to give... all taken from him. His family grieves for generations to come, gone from them an uncle, a brother, also a son.

In this dungeon, Shawn goes through the many trials and tribulations, his pain becomes evident. He talks to himself and asks why. Why did he want to follow the ruffians? Why did he feel so empty inside?

He knows now. Shawn wanted what every child desired. Love. He thought that he did not have it. All along he did. In his selfishness he chose to ignore it. The symptoms of being a kid.

Here now in this concrete dungeon he learns his worth. Through the legendary talking circles, magic and spirits abound as he heals his soul. Love and laughter, pain and sorrow, here in a safe place together for the first time, face to face. It is through this tireless trek he will become the man that he knows he could be.

That boy killed, that boy jailed, Shawn seeks to change in the depths of hell. Change into the man the world needs. Into the man in the mirror he wants to see. Forever in his heart he feels the pain of taking the life of another boy. So he lives his life in dedication to him.

From fields to a dungeon, I have never been so free. My journey has made me the things that I need to be. If another day passes that I cannot grow, I will see to it that the rest of the children will know. That it's ok to feel how you feel. You must not allow these emotions to direct your fear. For it is within you, all that you seek. I go to my community, a keeper of it, I must be.

Letter to a Young Homie

Oliver "Duck" Thomas

Hey little homie cuz, how old are you now? Cuz, you're 12 already. I remember when those motherfucken bloods killed your pops; you wasn't even one yet, lil nigga. Cuz, your pops was puttin in work and havin his lil scrilla. Yeah, pops was a down nigga. Lil homie, I know you're ready to rep your pops now cuz. Cuz you're a lil monster.

Hey little brother, how old are you now? Lil brother, you're 12 already. I remember when your pops passed, you were just a newborn. You know I met your pops when we were both 12 years old. We both were squares, he had lost his dad to gun violence and lost my dad to police violence. They had pulled him over and when they asked for his license, he reached for a gun. At least, that's what was told to me. I wasn't even a year old when it happened. Anyways, I hope little brother you're keeping your nose clean and making A's and B's in school. Lil brother, with a good education you can be who you choose to be and have what you want and go wherever you want to go.

Lil monster cuz, I seen you talking to that square-ass nigga. Duck: fuck that nigga cuz, he ain't with the business. Lil monster, jump in the low low and come with me for this drop. Then we're going to this house party. There's going to be plenty of homies, bitches, drink, and weed there, lil nigga. Yeah cuz, lil monster is gonna get him some pussy tonight and put on the set, feel me?

What's going on lil brother? I saw you get into Psycho's car with him. Lil brother, that's dangerous. Psyco is the drop-off man for the dope dealers and gun slangers. You can end up dead or in prison pushing with him. I heard that there was a shootout at the house party that he was at last night. A stray bullet struck and killed a 3-year-old three houses away. I got two tickets to the Lakers game tonight. Go ask your mother if you can go. Stay focused, lil bro.

Lil monster cuz, check what I got for my lil nigga. That's a .357 magnum, my nigga. That strap will blow a nigga's chest from him shoulders in one blow, cuz. And you know I can't have little monster running through these streets broke my nigga. Cuz, here is a couple of ounces. Nigga you ready to ball? Watch out for One Time and those haters because its nigga hunting season.

Hey lil brother, at the Lakers game last night, I talked to the manager of the Staples Center. He informed me that they were going to be giving summer jobs to 12 year olds and up. They will also be conducting a mentoring class run by the

Lakers. I got an application for you and I'll buy a bike for you to get to work and class on time.

Cuz, look at my lil nigga. You got latest Jordan kicks, sweats, the rollie chain, and pinky ring. Cuz, my lil nigga, lil moster is balllllllling! Nigga you 16 and having money now, that bitch Porsche talking 'bout she knocked up by you my nigga. All the homies tossed that up, cuz. I guess you wasn't shooting blanks cuz. Ain't the both of you the same age.

Lil Brother, you're 16 now and should have only 1 more year of school. It's time to really focus on what you want to become and have in this world. Now little brother, don't you go and get your little girlfriend pregnant. If you're going there, put a jacket on little brother. You know how hard it was for you and your mother.

We interrupt the Laker game to bring you breaking news. A 16-year-old was shot and killed.

In the news today, a 16-year-old young man was given a full scholarship to attend USC.

You *decide* which *one* is *the* real *news* and *which* one *is* the *fake* news.

(Dedicated to all the gang members of California and the world)

Humility

Robert Mosley IV

Living life in many places,

Avoid the pits as you pass through mazes.

Only given one try to master the place,

Do not get distracted by defining the race.

Chart you course with each heartbeat.

Use your soul and mind to direct your feet.

Travel light for you must go far.

The end you have will tell who you are.

Give praise for all,

Look for inspiration.

Do not call any bad,

Just a situation.

See it for the benefit it is,

For everything you get is a blessing of HIS.

You do not question a reflexive act.

Train yourself to rely on fact.

You may think it pain,

But, it does not, physically, really hurt.

Those that do not feel, now, are in the dirt.

As long as you can think and move,

To and fro',

Keep track of which way you go.

There is pleasure in life,

That is a given.

All you need do is keep on living.

Piety, sobriety, charity

And chaste of thought and deed,

Generate no waste.

Consider these things

When you want to grumble:

The winner is usually the one

That is truly humble.

Sing

Eric Nicholson

Sing a song of truth, sing proud and strong – sing for the old and new – sing of me – sing of you.

Sing that all may hear – of struggles of the past – sing your message through.

Sing for the weak and the strong – sing loud and true.

Sing away the pain – sing for hope and joy – sing for our nation;

every man, woman, girl and boy.

Sing of the lost – and remember the dead – as we sing of the grind and getting ahead.

Sing of our soul – sing of our faith – sing of our hope - sing of our grace.

Sing to smile – sing to cry – sing from our birth – Until our time to die.

Sing for our love – sing for self – sing for the memory of our cultural wealth.

Sing of the glory still locked inside – regardless of the truth they attempted to hide.

Lift your voices high in one regard – so the world may once again receive the message of God.

Sing, sing, sing of me – sing of you.

Liberated Syllables

Samual Nathaniel Brown

Wordz uncaged, wordz uncaged; Lights, camera, action the whole world is a stage/ These are, wordz uncaged, wordz un – ...what exactly are words uncaged? Are they like consonants and vowels on the prowl that *GRRROWLLL*, searching for a mind to invade? Are they...liberated syllables, freedoms to folic phonetically; Perhaps they're an opportunity to remorsefully and apologetically express the regret for the pain that we caused when we incessantly lived life so selfishly and disrespectfully.../Definitely, the latter.

The very ladder which we climb to rise above the mire, to rise above the fire; To rise from the ashes with wings of flames and the desire to fly higher.../Than we have ever flown before; On the winds of change we soar, above the clouds of trauma that clouded our judgment, but never no more/ I say, nah-nah never no mo', backwards I'm never gon' go; And much love to the horticulturist of consciousness who plant seeds in the minds of hardheads while brushing off the popular assertion that their neva' gon gro'/ 'Cause we are not incorrigible/ And Words Uncaged are not just words...

They're sculptures, drawings, multimedia masterpieces, stories told in oil and acrylic; they are symbols worth thousands of words, they are Bare Bones admissions of guilt so authentic that when you hear it you haf'ta feel it/ They're visions of Men for Honor, they're kaw-kaw! And peace; They're cohort 1, cohort 2, and California State University Los Angeles Professors using academia to shed light inside the belly of the beast/ They're American Sign Language, Youth STAND UP! 10Ps, and bachelor's degrees, these...

Wordz Uncaged, Wordz Uncaged; Freedom form depression, oppression, and suppressing rage/ These are Wordz Uncaged, Wordz Uncaged; Excuse me, but I feel compelled to expound and expand on the definition in efforts of ensuring that we are all on the same page/They're like...

Exonerated expressions, exculpatory emissions; Eclectically erected in efforts of effectively effectuating escape from eternal entrapment ergo egregious and erroneous decisions, exclamation!/ EZ to say, I say, but not so easy to live; And these uncaged words are but the tip of the iceberg of what we have to give, now that we realize the folly of the decisions we made when we were kids/ And all the wrong we did and me...I did a lot of bad; It came off as a lot of anger, but that was a poor attempt to disguise a lot of sad/ And I was very sad/ Because somewhere along the line I was taught to betray myself, that is, to be my own worst enemy; That is, to turn my back on the inner me, so eventually, I statistically, became another case of criminality rooted in emotional illiteracy...

O-M-Geezy/ Are you pizicking izup what I'm pizutting dizown?; And if sizo how in the wizorld does that sizound, for baseline, socio-economic, ethnographic, cutting-edge, criminogenic supposition?/ I mean listen, Emotional-Illiteracy Based Criminality; That means before I was an offender, I was a casualty/ So I didn't mean to offend'ya when I casually, reenacted the trauma that I silently suffered when I thought the whole world was mad at me/ So I was mad at the whole world, 'cause I thought the whole world hated me so I hated the whole world; As my development stopped, and my head twirled, my brain cooked as my blood burled, what ailed me I couldn't unfurl 'cause to talk about it was to be a little…

That is, according to the roles that were set forth for me by American Structural Functionalism/ You know, the patrilineal, ultra-masculine, super macho, real-men-don't-cry-crap, that socialized me to a standstill; Methodical as a planned kill, how my neglected emotions withered and dried like a mandrel/ That died, curled, and lied in an emotional landfill, with a stench which could make any man ill, and not a regular ill, but a grand ill, so damn ill, it couldn't be healed by a mil' in Advil; Had me down on my knees composing prayerful songs to the Messiah like George Handel/Hallelujah!!!

Other times I was just pissed, pouting, lips poked out like a dang Mandrill; That's real, my thoughts were like anvils/ That weighed on my brain 'cause they were heavy on my mind; However, as they slipped from my tongue they'd disintegrate, into the atmosphere with the intent to disseminate, a message of redemption to all of humankind:

"There are more people in prison than there are incarcerated"

But their sentences aren't commutated; On the contrary their freedom is orchestrated through due season words articulated/ Prison is, my mother used to smoke crack, now she smokes meth, my uncle does heroin; The molestation begin when I was ten, ever since then I dreaded leaving school and going back home/ My auntie is an angry alcoholic, my pops has never been there, my life has never been fair; My sister is a teen mother, my other one ran away, my brothers a gangbanga 'cause our other one got blown away, and it's like the world ain't never care/ And sheeeiiitt, I'm always scared, but I'll neva let it show; I've been raped, I've been robbed, I've been turned down for a job, but I know, I know that's just how it go/ Happens to us all right? So I guess that makes it alright, right? Wrong!

Hear this, it is not alright; And you do not have to embrace a soft death because you live a hard life/ Discover the medication that resides within your tribulation, word to the Troubadour; The potential for healing resides in the past traumas that you choose to explore/ It's called narrative therapy and Dr. Roy is big on it/ In the Dragon Klan, we call it The Work; Finding the heal in the hurt and I posit that Every Narrative is Seven Stories Tall/ There is…

(1) **The Story that I was born into**; Because the world, this

nation, my people, our culture, my family, my parents, already had their own stuff that they were going through/

(2) **The story of what happened to me**, the many faces of ACES; as in the Adverse Childhood Experiences I grew up faced with/

(3) Reflects my intrapersonal skills, **the story I tell myself**; Did I deserve it, should I pretend it didn't happen, is it cool to discuss it with anyone else?/

(4) Interpersonal skills, **the story I tell others**; like "I've never been hurt, and never will be hurt 'cause I'm one super duper califragilisticexpialidotiuos uber uber duper baaaad mutha…

(5) **The story others tell me about me**; Like "you ain't nuth'n, you ain't neva been nuth'n, and you ain't neva gon' be nuth'n, so don't try'ta neva' be nuth'n 'cause nuth'n is all you eva gon'be/ Yeah right…

(6) The story that I create through my decisions; And

(7) **The story that will be told about me when I am no longer living/**

Pick up that pen and write a new narrative, free yourself from that prison…/ of implosions of emotional volcanic eruptions in which you keep your piece; Mourning a relationship that you are still in because every day its filled with grief/ Black eyes, bruised cheeks, swollen lips, and loose teeth; working the most, but feeling appreciated the least…

Why are you waiting for a bully to cut you loose; from their spiritual, mental, verbal, sexual, and physical abuse?/ I will **NOT** wait for you to relinquish your control over me; I-HERE-BY-SET-ME-FREE:

> I TAKE back my power, ♛
> I TAKE back my control; ♛
> I TAKE back my spirit, ♀
> I TAKE back my soul… ♀

I'm free from being trapped by the traumatizing things to each other that we do; ☠

W o r d z U n c a g e d **are…**

Ase, I see you, #METOO/

'Cause secrets have power as long as you keep them a secret; But the second you begin to speak it the power of the secret weakens/ So don't be sitting there weeping keeping in something that hurts yourself; If you ever need help, then you ask someone for help/ And if that someone can't help, then you ask somebody else; And somebody else, and somebody else, until you find somebody who can help/Holding it in is bad for your health, this is spiritual bling bling – mental wealth; And you ain't gotta hurt nobody else in order for you to feel good about yourself/

So Dear Mr. President, why'ont'chu please try'ta see; That there'sa million billion jillion gazillion other people stressing just like me/ All around the world and across the clear blue sea; There are more people in prison than there are in the penitentiary/...waiting...dying...to be set free; by the words that reside inside of you and me...these Wordz Uncaged.

In Loving Memory Of All The Dead

Forgiveness
Ricardo Garcia

Giving Up All Hope for a Better Past: A Mother's Story of Forgiveness

Aba Gail

I sit and look through the pile of newspapers, magazines, and books that have all printed my story of loss and healing through forgiveness, and I wonder if anyone has read them. I haven't noticed any change in the prevailing world view of retribution and revenge. The articles have not made a difference that I can see or feel.

So, it is time to get this story out to more people. I must let people know that the way to heal their hearts and bodies is through forgiveness. It's the only way to reclaim personal power. And if we can teach individuals, groups, and governments the changes in perception that will allow them to heal old hurts and injustices, we will all find ourselves in a more peaceful world. This is the stand I'm taking, no matter the obstacle or outcome. Forgiveness is not something you give to someone else. Forgiveness is a gift you give yourself.

I

By all definitions I am a victim, because I am the mother of a beautiful young daughter who was brutally murdered. But I have learned that I have a choice in how to live. So I've chosen to stop being a victim...and this has not been an easy road. My story began one Monday in October, 1980. I had been to the California State Department of Waterways to give a short sales pitch and answer questions about the HMO I worked for. Suddenly, I felt something was wrong. I didn't know what, but I had the distinct sensation of something unpleasant. This feeling settled in my stomach and I decided to spend my lunch hour resting at home. I walked into my house and immediately heard the phone ringing. I picked up the phone and the voice at the other end of the line said, "Well, what do you think about Catherine being shot?"

"What do you mean? What are you talking about?" I asked.

"Well, haven't you heard? Catherine was shot!"

I quickly got off the phone and called the Placer County Sheriff's Department and said, "This is Gayle, mother of Catherine Blount. I hear she has been shot. What hospital is she in? How is she? I am her mother. She needs me. I must go to her!"

The voice at the other end of the line obviously didn't want to have to talk to me. He said, "No, ma'am, your daughter hasn't been shot. Your daughter is dead.

I will have someone call you right back."

I know what it's like to be temporarily insane.

I waited for the phone to ring. My body was tense and tight and there was a tingling pain all over. I paced from room to room. I never drank tea, but that afternoon I drank a whole pot and then made another. I seem to have left my body and time had stood still. I was frozen in my pain. I happened to glance up at the wall clock. Three long, long hours had gone by. I could wait no longer. I picked up the phone and called the Place County Sheriff's Department again. This time I simply said, "Someone must speak to me right now or I will lose my mind." Finally, Detective Landry came on the line. He was as kind and gentle as possible as he spoke these terrible words to me.

"I am sorry but your daughter Catherine is dead. Your daughter Catherine was murdered. She was stabbed to death."

Something in me broke. My brain couldn't think. I had to remain calm. None of this day was real. Soon I would wake up and the nightmare would be over, but deep down I knew it was real. I couldn't let anyone hug me; I was afraid I could break down. I couldn't cry; someone might hear me. I decided to take a shower and with the water running full blast, I screamed, and screamed, and screamed. Sometimes, in order to survive this life, you do just what you have to do to keep your head above water. My method of survival was to be calm and not cause anyone any problems. I had no support system. I had to remain strong to help everyone else.

I was alone.

My mother was recovering from open-heart surgery and she was very fragile. I had to protect her from my pain; I couldn't allow her to see how much I was suffering. My father was busy taking care of my mom and unable to talk about Catherine without crying. My son and daughter, Catherine's older brother and sister, had just left for medical school far away. I couldn't burden them with my tears – they had enough to do to endure with their own pain, as they began 4-plus years of grueling medical training.

About six weeks after Catherine's death, my husband, Catherine's step father, announced that he didn't want to talk about Catherine anymore. He stated emphatically, that he did not intend to mourn her for the rest of his life. I didn't realize at the time how differently people mourn. I felt abandoned. There were acquaintances at my work who did not say a word to me. A couple of them had children who had gone to school with Catherine. It was as if Catherine had never existed. I have since learned that they were subconsciously afraid to acknowledge

Catherine's murder because doing so would make it real; and if it was real, it could possibly happen to them. So they chose to say nothing. And I was so hurt.

I found myself more and more isolated, with no one to give me the love and encouragement I needed so badly. For a while, I couldn't even drive my car alone because I would cry and couldn't see the road. The Placer County district attorney told me that the sheriff's department would find the person that murdered Catherine. The district attorney would put him on trial, get a guilty conviction, and make certain that the murderer would receive the death penalty. He assured me that when that horrible villain was executed, I would be healed of my pain and would be well again. And because I didn't know any other way to believe, I thought it was true.

II

Douglas Mickey was caught and arrested in Japan and tried in Redwood City, California. I attended one pretrial hearing in Auburn, California. It was so excruciatingly painful that I found myself sobbing. After the hearing, I stood outside the courtroom talking with Detective Landry. As we stood there, a sheriff's deputy walked out of the court with Douglas Mickey. Mickey stopped to say hello to Landry. Landry offered a brief condolence to Douglas about his father's recent death. Landry told me that he believed in prosecution, not persecution. I think I stopped breathing. Why didn't I lash out and beat on Mickey? Why didn't I scream at him? Why was I so civilized that I just stood there and said nothing? I was so afraid of losing control and going over the edge.

I decided not to attend the trial. I couldn't see any sense in inflicting further pain on myself. I was in enough pain already. My father represented Catherine's family at the trial. The only people at the sentencing were the district attorney, the sheriff, the psychiatrist who testified for the prosecution, one jury member and me. Douglas Mickey was sentenced to death. I was struck by the fact that the judge was going to sentence someone to death and no one cared. Not the press, not the jury, not the friends or family of the murderer.

At the same time, I didn't understand why he wasn't executed right away. Why did it take so long? Why couldn't I get rid of my pain? I didn't understand anything about the process of appeals and I resented every minute that he lived. As the mother of a victim, I was ignored and given no support. There were no victim services at the time. I inquired about support groups, but no one knew of any. The one psychiatrist I visited at the time simply handed me a book on losing a child and told me he hoped it might be of help. He told me that he had no experience in what had happened to me and didn't know what to say.

I went through all the normal stages of grieving. Uncontrollable crying would appear without warning. My mind could not totally accept that Catherine was gone I found myself in denial. One day I was shopping in Macy's and took a dress of the rack that I thought was the perfect color and size for Catherine. She would look darling in it, I thought. As I looked at the dress, I remembered that I didn't have Catherine anymore and I had to put the dress back. My shopping was over for the day.

When I reached the anger stage, I got stuck. On the surface I looked okay. Had you known me at the time, you wouldn't have known about the dark, ugly cloud I carried around inside. You would have thought I was getting along just fine, but a deep dark rage began to boil. There was an awful, hideous darkness, and all I wanted was revenge for the death of my beloved child. It lasted eight years.

And   then,   unknowingly,   the   healing   began.

III

I was given a free lesson in meditation by a friend at the Berkeley Psychic Institue. I started the classes without any reason or goals. It was close to home; it gave me an excuse to be out once a week; and meditation was the one spiritual practice that my husband didn't think was stupid and that I therefore didn't have to defend. The first night of class, the teacher had us all arrange our chairs in a circle and instructed us to go around and say our names and tell a little about what we expected to get out of the class. When it was my turn, I told them my name and said I had no idea why I was there. There was a man sitting to the left of me whom I'd never seen before in my life. He leaned over and whispered in my ear, "I know what you will get out of this class. You will get faith." I thought, what does he know? He doesn't know what happened to me. I thought his comment was ridiculous.

I found the class to be very interesting; certainly, everything was brand new to me. I stayed with that class for over a year and it brought some profound changes into my life. I found myself able to sit quietly. I learned to quiet and to listen for my inner voice. I learned to be in the present and not always evaluate everything by my past experiences. For the first time in my life, I realized that I did not have to see, touch, or even hear something to know that it was real. I learned there is far more to this universe than our own senses perceive. I had found a faith and a power outside of myself. The man sitting next to me at the first session had been right.

IV

My parents were married for over fifty years. Their life was an ongoing romance.

When my father died of lung cancer, my mom tried to carry on her life. But her failing health had left her quite fragile and unable to cope with living alone. I was blessed to be able to live with and to care for her. We knew that Mom probably had another two years of life left because of her artificial mitral valve. I was determined that these would be two of the best years of her life. My brother and I took her out for lunch every Sunday afternoon. I hired young women to take her shopping and out to lunch during the week. Then I remembered that my mom and dad had attended the Unity Church in downtown Sacramento. I didn't want to take mom on such a long drive on the freeway. I looked around and found a beautiful little Unity church in Auburn, California. It was only a twenty-minute drive from our home up the Auburn Folsom Road and it was beautiful at all times of the year.

So I started taking mom to church every Sunday. She loved the drive and being in church and enjoyed the coffee and cake after the service as much as anything. I simply sat through the service. I was only there for my mother. After several weeks of attending church, I finally raised my eyes to the front and saw a beautiful vision named Billie Blain. She was the minister and everything she talked about that day was exactly what i needed to hear. The next week the same thing happened. I got interested and started paying attention.

Then I discovered the church's bookstore. Here I found books on Christianity, Buddhism, Hinduism, Bahai, Judaism, mythology and other books on the lives and teachings of great religious and philosophical leaders. I also found self-help books by authors like Wayne Dyer, Richard Bach, and Louise Hays. I love to read and usually read a book a week. This bookstore was a challenge because I didn't know where to start or what books to pick. Luckily, I was befriended by Billie's husband, Wes Blain, who became my own personal librarian. Every week he would recommend a book and I would come back the following week and we would talk about and he would recommend another. I read and studied my way through that book store.

You can't read your way through a metaphysical bookstore without having some major changes occur in your spirit/soul. I learned that I am a beloved child of God, that I am one with the universe, and that all of us are here to love each other, without exception. God is a loving God and there is no hell except that which we create in our own minds. I really "got it" that we are all one in spirit. I fell in love with God. One day Reverend Billie announced that she would be facilitating a class based on the book, A Course in Miracles. I signed up. We watched a video about how the book was written and the history of the people involved. It was while watching this video that I got my first glimpse of the healing power of forgiveness. It showed several interviews with people who studied A Course in Miracles. One of the men was a Jewish Holocaust survivor. He was able to forgive not only the German people, but also the actual guards in the camps who had killed every member of his family. Something in me clicked when I heard that testimony. I began to feel that perhaps I could forgive the man who killed Catherine. A seed was planted in my heart.

The time came when I was no longer able to take care of my mom and carry on with my work. My son-in-law invited my mother to live with his family in Santa Rosa. I was able to find a townhouse less than a mile from their home. Between my daughter (who was now a family practice physician), my grandchildren's nanny, Helen, the angels from Hospice and myself, we were able to keep my mom at home. She loved watching movies with her great-granddaughter Catherine and great-grandson Connor. (It is a blessing to all involved to be able to keep our loved ones at home and not have to turn their care over to strangers.) When Mom died, it was in a familiar room with all her own furniture and family pictures.

I continued attending a study group for A Course in Miracles. Because the group met in the same building, I also began attending the Santa Rosa Church of Religious Science and began taking classes to study Science of the Mind by Ernest Holmes. This is where I met my next two teachers, Reverend Mary Murry Shelton, the church's minister, and Reverend Karyl Huntly, the assistant minister. Karyl was my teacher for the first class called Foundations One. One thing we all knew at the end of the class was that Karyl loved us. One of Karyl's classes focused on forgiveness. I was sure I had done all my forgiveness work. I thought I had forgiven. I was soon to realize that what I thought was forgiveness was head-centered and not heart-centered. One of my classmates announced that she knew that forgiveness wasn't real unless you let the person know he/she is forgiven. I was outraged that she could expect me to visit that monster in San Quentin Prison who had murdered my Catherine. It turned into a verbal melee, and I am grateful that Reverend Karyl was our teacher and calmed us down and assured me that I did not have to visit because I wasn't ready. My classmate-now a close friend-wound up sitting next to me in tears because she didn't know about my loss. That night another seed was planted in my heart.

One day when I was trying to figure out what wonderful project I could create for the class, I received a letter from a friend in Auburn with a newspaper clipping stating that Douglas Mickey's execution had been scheduled. All the forgiveness that I had been carrying around in my head vanished, just like a crystal glass thrown on a cement floor. I immediately called San Quentin and demanded that I be allowed as a witness. I discovered the newspaper had made a mistake; there was no execution scheduled on the date stated. But I was instructed to write a letter to the warden and request I be notified when there was a date set for Mickey's execution. This I did. I put the letter on my desk and prepared to go to class. It was never mailed.

I went to class with a feeling of nervous expectation. I didn't have a project for the following week, and I was feeling frustrated. I felt I was letting myself and Reverend Mary down with my lack of creativity. After class I drove home going north on Mendocino Avenue. I was directly in front of the junior college when I distinctly heard a voice. It said, "YOU MUST FORGIVE HIM AND YOU MUST LET HIM KNOW!" The voice was so loud and clear, and so persuasive, that it didn't let me sleep that night. I was compelled to get out of bed at four a.m. and type a letter to the man who murdered Catherine. The letter said:

Dear Mr. Mickey,

Twelve years ago I had a beautiful daughter named Catherine. She was a young woman of unusual talents and intelligence. She was slender, and her skin glowed with health and vitality. She had long naturally wavy hair that framed her sparkling eyes and warm bright smile. She radiated love and joy.

Catherine was living with her friend Eric on a fifteen-acre pear ranch. Catherine's greatest love was her animals. She was raising two milk goats, her German shepherd with a new litter of ten puppies and an Arabian mare. She had tried to live with her father and his wife on their property (where there would be room for all her animals) but her stepmother's emotional illness made that impossible and she had just recently moved back with her friend Eric.

Two months after her 19th birthday Catherine left her earthly body and her spirit transitioned to her next stage of life. I know that Catherine is in a better place that we can never know here on Earth. I did not know that when Catherine died. I knew that I had been robbed of my precious child and that she had been robbed of growing into womanhood and achieving all of her potential. The violent way she left this Earth was impossible for me to understand. I was saddened beyond belief and felt that I would never be completely happy again. And indeed, my loss of Catherine became the point of reference for my entire family. All family history was prefaced as happening either before or after Catherine's death.

I was very angry with you and wanted to see you punished to the limit of the law. You had done irreparable damage to my family and my dreams for the future.

After eight long years of grief and anger, I started my journey of life. I met wonderful teachers and slowly began to learn about my Gold-self. In the midst of a class studying A Course in Miracles, I was surprised to find that I could forgive you. This does not mean that I think you are innocent or that you are blameless for what happened. What I learned is this: You are a divine child of God. You carry the Christ consciousness within you. You are surrounded by God's love even as you sit in your cell. There is no devil; there is only the goodness of God. The Christ in me sends blessings to the Christ in you.

Do not look to me to be a political or social advocate on your behalf. The law of the land will determine your fate. Do not waste your last days on Earth with remorse or fear. Death as we know it is really a new beginning. Hell does not exist except in our conscious minds.

I hope that this letter will help you to face your future. There is only love and good in the world, regardless of how things may appear to you now. I am willing to write to you or visit you if you wish. I send blessings to you and to your children.

Gayle, Mother of Catherine

I stood before my class to read the letter. After the first sentence, Reverend Mary asked me to stop so she could distribute Kleenex to the class. I resumed reading. When I finished the entire class rose to their feet and embraced me with tears and love. It was because of this outpouring of love and support that I was able to mail the letter. It is one thing to write a letter like this. It is something else altogether to mail it. Shivers still go up and down my spine as I remember the little "click" that the hinged mail box made as I dropped the letter in. When I heard it, all the anger, all the rage, all the lust for revenge vanished in an instant. In its place, I was filled with the most incredible feeling of joy and love and peace. I was in a state of grace. I knew in that instant I did not need to have anyone executed for me to be healed. I could now get on with my life.

It wouldn't have mattered if Douglas Mickey hadn't responded to my letter. I had received a more profound answer. I had been healed by the simple act of offering forgiveness. And this time it came from my heart, not my head. But I did get a letter back. And I was totally amazed at the gentleness and kindness of the writer. Douglas wrote back with words of gratitude. He expressed remorse and sorrow for the crime, also stating that he fully understood how empty such words might sound. I could tell from reading his letter that he was intelligent and well read. He had obviously spent years studying for answers himself. He wrote back, "The Christ in me most gratefully accepts and returns blessings of divine wisdom, love and charity to the Christ in you." He also said, "I would gladly give my life this instant if it would in any way change that terrible night."

Mickey invited me to visit and enclosed two visiting forms with his letter. He said that he realized how difficult it might be for me and suggested I come with a friend. It took ninety days to get permission from San Quentin to visit. During that time, Douglas and I exchanged many letters. I was amazed at the depth of his knowledge of A Course in Miracles, Ancient Egypt, Psychology and Carl Jung.

V

The day to visit came and all the people who had said they would accompany me were busy. I was on my own. I'd never even been near a prison when I visited Douglas at San Quentin. There I was, all alone, driving south on highway 101 from Santa Rosa to San Rafeal. It was after the commute time and on a weekday, so the traffic was relatively light. The anticipation of the meeting created butterflies in my stomach, light perspiration on my palms and a tremor in my knees. What was I doing? This was not what my mother had raised me to do! (I have since learned that the strength is always given to me). Just before the San Rafeal bridge, I turned into the road marked "San Quentin." This turned out to be a beautiful, scenic road along the edge of the San Fransisco Bay. A few old Victorian buildings and some new townhouses lined the road to the gates of the prison.

There were no signs. I drove up to the gates and asked the guard where to go and what to do. He politely directed me to the parking lot down a steep drive. Once more I was struck by the stark contrast of the beautiful bay with sailboats, the sunny freshness of everything. There was just the tease of San Fransisco, just across the bay. The Larkspur Ferry sailed past. It was a surreal experience. I parked the car and walked back up the drive to a rectangular building.

I entered a long, narrow hall that could have used a good cleaning. Again, no signs anywhere to show how or where to proceed. There was one door and I found it locked. After a few minutes, I heard a buzzing sound and heard the door would now open. There was a counter with two women guards behind it. I threw myself on their mercy and announced, "I have never been here before and I am terrified."

Their reply was, "Don't worry, we'll take care of you."

I placed my jewelry and shoes in a wooden box for inspection. I had been forewarned not to wear anything with metal on it (buttons, underwire bra, belt, etc.). I had no problem going through the metal detector. The guards found I had not been listed as an approved visitor. Luckily, I had brought my letter of approval with me. They sent me out a side door and I began the long walk to the next gate.

The visiting room for death row inmates was a large room with a capacity for eighty people. Everyone was seated in plastic chairs set in rows facing a glass booth where two guards were sitting. It was almost as if everyone was lined up to watch a play. There was one guard walking around the room. There were a couple of vending machines where you could buy overpriced soft drinks and candy bars. I looked around with surprise. I did not see a single monster in that room. It was filled with ordinary-looking men, perhaps neater and quieter than on the outside. They were sitting with their girlfriends, grandmothers, wives, ministers, priests, children.

I had to wait for forty-five minutes and became more and more afraid and nervous. Everywhere I looked I saw the face of God. I kept my eye on the door where inmates were coming in. Each time that strange metal-and-air noise came, I looked up and wondered, is this Douglas? Finally, a tall man with long hair came through the door. He walked up the guard station to check in and the guard pointed at me. Douglas walked over to where I was sitting and said, " Gayle, you do me the greatest honor by paying me this visit."

We talked together for over three hours. I cried, and he cried. He is a big, tall, very strong man and he wasn't the least bit embarrassed to sit there, surrounded by other inmates, and openly weep. We talked about Catherine. We talked about his mother and her death. We talked about his losses. I realized that the night Catherine lost her life, Douglas also lost his future. When I left San Quentin that day, after only one visit, I knew that I would never stop spreading the word that these men were human beings and not monsters. I knew that I would be a political and social advocate on their behalf. And I knew that if the state of California ever executed Douglas Mickey, they would be killing my friend.

I now refer to the time I spend visiting men on death row as my "mini prison ministry." When asked by reporters if any of the men on death row have committed crimes that are just too awful for me to treat them with compassion, I respond, "I don't deal with the crime. I don't deal with that part of them. I deal with the God-Spirit within him or her. That is the truth of their being. It is the truth for everyone of us." Before Catherine's murder, I had never thought one way or another about the death penalty. I was Kappa Kappa Gamma at the University of Wisconsin, raised to be an upper middle class housewife. My mother certainly didn't raise me to go visit men on death row. For most of the twelve years after Catherine was killed, I would have been insulted if someone had suggested that Douglas Mickey was a human being, and not some kind of horrible monster.

I knew when I dropped the letter in the mailbox that I must spend the rest of my life demonstrating that killing was not necessary, and the violence begets only violence. I have learned that healing and grace can be achieved by anyone, under any circumstance, through the miracle of forgiveness. This may have appeared to be a new paradigm to me as I began this healing journey, but it is actually the universal truth that has been given to all people through sacred teachings such as those expressed by Jesus, the Buddha, Baha'u'llah, Mohammed, and other enlightened beings, and in many sacred writings.

I know my daughter Catherine is happy. I am honoring her with this work. She would not want me to go through life full of hate and rage. Love and forgiveness is the only way to make our world a kinder, safer place. And it begins with me.

Photo Index

Photographs by F. Scott Schafer

Special Thanks
From the men of Lancaster Prison

Mr. Ronald Underwood...our education department's fearless leader. Thank you for all your support and efforts, without you, this journal would not be possible. Thank you for spending hours on end in the computer lab with us while we bothered you with incessant "prints" (we may be responsible for more than several of your white hairs). Your patience, kindness, and spirit helped create the positive environment in which hundreds of men are bettering themselves through education. We appreciate all that you do and we cannot thank you enough.

Mr. J.D. Hughes...our Cal State Liaison. You have been invaluable as we coordinated with Cal State Los Angeles in the process of creating this journal. When we needed a clutch, 4th quarter, last 3 seconds of the game shooter, you have always came through for us. You have been a mentor and always treated us with respect. Thank you for your encouragement and support. We all appreciate you.

Professor Bidhan Roy...you are a visionary. We have told you this repeatedly and while you are too modest to ever accept the title, it is what you are. Seeing how things should be, how they can be improved, how a person is, and how to make them better—those are the gifts of every visionary throughout history and those are qualities you possess. Your ability to see the world as better than it may appear to the rest of us does not mean we do not share your hopes for the future—we do. We believe in you, and know you believe in us. Thank you.

Cal State LA Student Editorial Staff...without you, none of this would be possible. It is cliché, true enough, but appropriate. Your helpful edits, honest feedback, insightful opinions, inspiring suggestions, thoughtful questions, and overall literary wisdom helped us in numerous ways beyond simply "fixing our mistakes." You took the time to guide us through the maze of good writing—we thank you from the deepest corners of our hearts.